DOCTOR OF THE CHURCH

To Frances and Clive, Andrew and Janette, David and Sawa

DOCTOR OF THE CHURCH

AN INTRODUCTION TO
Saint John Henry Newman

Michael Rear

WITH A PREFACE BY
His Majesty King Charles III

GRACEWING

First published as *Blessed John Henry Newman*
St Paul's Publishing, 2010

Revised edition
Doctor of the Church: An Introduction to Saint John Henry Newman
First published in England in 2025
by
Gracewing
2 Southern Avenue
Leominster
Herefordshire HR6 0QF
United Kingdom
www.gracewing.co.uk

ISBN 978 085244 951 6

Cover image:
Mosaic by Tom Phillips in Westminster Cathedral,
used by kind permission.

Cover design by Bernardita Peña Hurtado

Typeset by Word and Page, Chester, UK

CONTENTS

ACKNOWLEDGEMENTS

My thanks for their help to Catherine Rear, Margaret Hulme and David Chapman

PREFACE

by His Majesty King Charles III

John Henry Newman: The Harmony of Difference

WHEN POPE FRANCIS canonises Cardinal John Henry Newman tomorrow, the first Briton to be declared a saint in over forty years, it will be a cause of celebration not merely in the United Kingdom, and not merely for Catholics, but for all who cherish the values by which he was inspired. In the age when he lived, Newman stood for the life of the spirit against the forces that would debase human dignity and human destiny. In the age in which he attains sainthood, his example is needed more than ever—for the manner in which, at his best, he could advocate without accusation, could disagree without disrespect and, perhaps most of all, could see differences as places of encounter rather than exclusion.

At a time when faith was being questioned as never before, Newman, one of the greatest theologians of the nineteenth century, applied his intellect to one of the most pressing questions of our era: what should be the relationship of faith to a sceptical, secular age? His engagement first with Anglican theology, and then, after his conversion, Catholic theology, impressed even his opponents with its fearless honesty, its unsparing rigour and its originality of thought. Whatever our own beliefs, and no matter what our own tradition may be, we can only be grateful to Newman for the gifts, rooted in his Catholic faith, which he shared with wider society: his intense and moving spiritual autobiography and his deeply felt poetry in *The Dream of Gerontius* which, set to music by Sir Edward Elgar—another Catholic of whom all Britons can be proud—gave the musical world one of its most enduring choral masterpieces. At the climax of *The Dream of Gerontius* the soul, approaching heaven, perceives something of the divine vision: a grand mysterious harmony. It floods me, like the deep and solemn sound of many waters. Harmony requires difference. The concept rests at the very heart of Christian theology in the concept of the Trinity. In the same poem, Gerontius says: 'Firmly I believe and truly God is three, and God is One'; as such, difference is not to be feared. Newman not only proved this in his theology and illustrated it in his poetry, but he also demonstrated it in his life. Under his leadership, Catholics became fully part of the wider society, which itself thereby became all the richer as a community of communities.

Newman engaged not merely with the Church, but with the world. While wholeheartedly committed to the Church to which he came through so many intellectual and spiritual trials, he nonetheless initiated open debate between Catholics and other Christians, paving the way for later ecumenical dialogues. On his elevation to the Cardinalate in 1879, he took as his motto *Cor ad cor loquitur* (heart speaks to heart), and his conversations across confessional, cultural, social and economic divides, were rooted in that intimate friendship with God.

His faith was truly catholic in that it embraced all aspects of life. It is in that same spirit that we, whether we are Catholics or not, can, in the tradition of the Christian Church throughout the ages, embrace the unique perspective, the particular wisdom and insight, brought to our universal experience by this one individual soul. We can draw inspiration from his writings and his life even as we recognise that, like all human lives, it was inevitably flawed. Newman himself was aware of his failings, such as pride and defensiveness, which fell short of his own ideals, but which, ultimately, left him only more grateful for the mercy of God. His influence was immense. As a theologian, his work on the development of doctrine showed that our understanding of God can grow over time, and had a profound impact on later thinkers.

Individual Christians have found their personal devotion challenged and strengthened by the importance he attached to the voice of conscience. Those of all traditions who seek to define and defend Christianity have found themselves grateful for the way he reconciled faith and reason. Those who seek the divine in what can seem like an increasingly hostile intellectual environment find in him a powerful ally who championed the individual conscience against an overwhelming relativism.

And perhaps most relevantly of all at this time, when we have witnessed too many grievous assaults by the forces of intolerance on communities and individuals, including many Catholics, because of their beliefs, he is a figure who stood for his convictions despite the disadvantages of belonging to a religion whose adherents were denied full participation in public life. Through the whole process of Catholic emancipation and the restoration of the Catholic Church hierarchy, he was the leader his people, his church and his times needed. His capacity for personal warmth and generous friendship is shown in his correspondence. There exist over thirty collected volumes of his letters, many of which, tellingly, are not addressed to the fellow intellectuals and prominent leaders but to family, friends and parishioners who sought out his wisdom.

His example has left a lasting legacy. As an educator, his work was profoundly influential in Oxford, Dublin and beyond, while his treatise, *The Idea of a University*, remains a defining text to this day. His often-over-looked labours on behalf of children's education are testimony to his commitment to ensuring those of all backgrounds shared the opportunities learning can bring. As an Anglican, he guided that Church back to its Catholic roots, and as a Catholic he was ready to learn from the Anglican tradition, such as in his promoting the role of the laity. He gave the Catholic Church renewed confidence as it re-established itself in a land from which it had once been uprooted. The Catholic community in Britain today owes an incalculable debt to his tireless work, even as British society has cause for gratitude to that community for its immeasurably valuable contribution to our country's life. That confidence was expressed in his love of the English landscape and of his native country's culture, to which he made such a distinguished contribution.

In the Oratory which he established in Birmingham, and which now houses a museum dedicated to his memory as well as an active worshipping community, we see the realisation in England of a vision he derived from Rome which he described as 'the most wonderful place on Earth'. In bringing the Oratorian Congregation from Italy to England, Newman sought to share its charism of education and service. He loved Oxford, gracing it not only with passionate and erudite sermons, but also with the beautiful Anglican church at Littlemore, created after a formative visit to Rome where, seeking guidance on his future spiritual path and pondering his relationship with the Church of England and with Catholicism, he wrote his beloved hymn, 'Lead Kindly Light'. When he finally decided to leave the Church of England, his last sermon as he said farewell to Littlemore left the congregation in tears. It was entitled 'The Parting of Friends'.

As we mark the life of this great Briton, this great churchman and, as we can now say, this great saint, who bridges the divisions between traditions, it is surely right that we give thanks for the friendship which, despite the parting, has not merely endured, but has strengthened. In the image of divine harmony which Newman expressed so eloquently, we can see how, ultimately, as we follow with sincerity and courage the different paths to which conscience calls us, all our divisions can lead to a greater understanding and all our ways can find a common home.

Lecture given by His Royal Highness Prince Charles on the eve of the canonisation of John Henry Newman in Rome, 12 October 2019.

Newman possessed a sort of prophetic charisma, as one who, because he knew of only two absolutely luminous realities, God and his own soul, was able not only to diagnose the evils of his own day but to see beyond them to the abiding purposes of the God of our salvation.

Bishop Christopher Butler OSB

The characteristic of the great Doctor of the Church, it seems to me, is that he teaches not only through his thought and speech, but rather by his life, because within him thought and life are interpenetrated and defined. If this is so, then Newman belongs to the great teachers of the Church, because at the same time he touches our hearts and enlightens our thinking.

Pope Benedict XVI

— 1 —

Newman's Early Years

OHN HENRY NEWMAN, pastor, theologian, teacher, writer, cardinal, saint and doctor of the Church: his life spanned most of the nineteenth century, yet he has been called a man for today. No one influenced the Church of England more than he during his lifetime: few have influenced the Catholic Church more since his death. And he continues to do so. His long life (1801–90) was spent almost equally in both Churches. The eldest of six children, three boys and three girls; their father was a London banker and their mother of French Huguenot descent. They were brought up in an undistinguished but gentle Anglican household, where the Bible and Catechism were read and the way of Christian living was firmly implanted. As a child, he tells us, he took 'great delight in reading the Bible'.

Conversion

The young John Henry, at the age of seven, became a boarder at the well-known Great Ealing School and stayed there until he went up to Oxford. He not only excelled academically, but learned to play the violin (very well) and compose. He acted in Latin plays, appreciated the Classics (especially the oratory of Cicero), edited several school magazines and enjoyed debating and speaking. His happy life was shattered however, when his father's bank closed in the economic crisis that hit Europe in the wake of the Napoleonic wars. To save him from the turmoil at home, his father asked him to stay on at school after the end of the Summer Term in 1816 (though the worry and loneliness of it made him ill). He later looked back on his illness as providential because it brought him into closer contact with his classics master, an evangelical clergyman Walter Mayers ('the human means of the beginning of divine faith in me', Newman wrote). He experienced an 'inward conversion' about which, even in his sixty-third year, he was able to confess, 'I still am more certain than that I have hands and feet'.

1

In the weeks following this conversion he sensed his calling in life would require celibacy, and that it could be missionary work to which he felt himself drawn. Writing about this many years later he thought celibacy 'also strengthened my feeling of separation from the visible world'.[1]

Mayers lent him several books by evangelical divines that had a profound and lasting effect on his young mind. One was Thomas Scott's *The Force of Truth*. Newman confessed that Scott 'made a deeper impression on my mind than any other, and to [him] (humanly speaking) I almost owe my soul'. It was from Scott that Newman learned what became central to his own teaching and growth; the importance of conscience as a moral guide, and obedience to the light of truth. He admired Scott's courageous obedience in converting from Unitarianism to belief in the Holy Trinity. From *The Force of Truth* he took the maxim, 'Holiness rather than peace', and this became a fundamental principle of his Christian life. He refused to settle for a state of spiritual or moral mediocrity, and consistently sought and prayed for holiness. Another influential book from Mayers was *The History of the Church of Christ* by Joseph Milner, who introduced Newman to the early Fathers of the Church, those bishops and theologians who lived immediately after the apostles; and who became his spiritual companions and study for the rest of his life. The New Testament, and these earliest interpreters of it, became the bedrock of Newman's theology and teaching.

Newman therefore owed a great deal to Evangelical Anglicanism, and although he moved away from it he remained ever grateful for it. In 1887 he wrote to the secretary of the London Evangelization Society:

> what should, what can I say, but that those great and burning truths, which I learned when a boy from evangelical teaching, I have found impressed upon my heart with fresh and ever-increasing force by the Holy Roman Church. That Church has added to the simple evangelicalism of my first teachers, but it has obscured nothing of it—on the contrary, I have found a power, a resource, a comfort, a consolation in our Lord's divinity and atonement, in His Real Presence, in communion in His Divine and Human Person, which all good Catholics indeed have, but which Evangelical Christians have but faintly.[2]

In similar vein he wrote that '[Evangelical] teaching had been a great blessing for England and brought home to thousands the cardinal and vital truths of revelation, to himself among others'.[3] Nevertheless, it was tainted with the Calvinist 'detestable doctrine' (as he later called it) that the elect are incapable of falling away, that the converted and the unconverted can be discriminated by man, and that the justified are conscious of their state of justification. 'St Paul did not divide his brethren into two, the converted and unconverted', he reflected. Another book lent by Mayers, Thomas Newton's *Dissertations on the Prophecies*, implanted a hostile attitude towards the Roman Catholic Church, convincing him that the pope was the anti-Christ. Such robust hostility is not easily dislodged.

> My imagination was stained by the effects of this doctrine up to the year 1843; it had been obliterated from my reason and judgment at an earlier date; but the thought remained upon me as a sort of false conscience.[4]

Many others in England have been misled into a similar antipathy and will know exactly what Newman meant.

— 2 —

Newman in Oxford

T HIS HIGHLY INTELLIGENT YOUNG MAN OF SIXTEEN, at a not unusual age in those days, went up to Trinity College, Oxford, in 1817. He proved to be a diligent student, though Trinity was not then one of the best Oxford colleges. 'I really think, if anyone should ask me what qualifications were necessary for Trinity College, I should say there was only one—drink, drink, drink.' But he much enjoyed going to concerts, attending lectures outside his own fields of study, and writing for the university magazine. His hard work paid off, for within a year he was awarded a nine-year Trinity scholarship. Through nervous anxiety he shocked everyone by spoiling his finals, failing in mathematics and achieving only a pass in classics: but he quickly retrieved the disaster in 1822 by winning a Fellowship to the intellectually eminent Oriel College. Fellows were expected to be ordained; a stipulation that did little to adorn the sacred ministry, but for Newman there was a true vocation within. On 13 June 1824 he was ordained deacon, and wrote in his journal:

> It is over. I am thine, Lord ... At first, after the hands were laid on me, my heart shuddered within me; the words 'for ever' are so terrible ... At times indeed my heart burned within me, particularly during the singing of the *Veni Creator*. Yet Lord, I ask not for comfort in comparison with sanctification.[1]

Next day he wrote, 'I have a responsibility of souls on me to the day of my death'. He truly meant this, and everything he did in his life, from preaching and teaching to writing his celebrated books; in all the controversies that ensued, this was his one end: the salvation of souls.

It was in a poor parish, St Clement's, just outside Oxford, his first experience of working-class poverty, that Newman took up his responsibility as a curate and prepared for the priesthood. Visiting his flock house by house; getting to know and love each person; he began to lose that hard, unreal distinction between the saved and the damned. In his sermons at St Clement's, he spoke frequently of holiness and heaven, as he would do constantly throughout his life, presenting virtue and holiness as the object and purpose of the Christian life.

> I have insisted much that the future reward of our present virtue is described as merely the *perfection and the completion* of that virtue—that the reward of attempting to do our duty will be the *power* of doing our duty entirely. Thus there is a *connexion* between this life and the next—between future holiness and future happiness—between obedience here and the reward of obedience hereafter.[2]

Crowds who came to hear him preach had to be turned away from the doors, and for two happy years he laboured at St Clement's, until at Easter 1826 he became a tutor of his college (which meant giving up the parish).

At about the same time, Richard Hurrell Froude, as ardent a catholic-minded Anglican as Newman was evangelical, was also appointed a tutor at Oriel. Churchmanship kept them apart, and it was more than a year before they became close friends. After that no one had more influence on Newman than he. One of the few Anglicans of the period to have a genuine understanding of the Church of Rome, he could not understand why Newman held it to be anti-Christian; and he it was who caused him to revise his ideas.

> I speak of Hurrell Froude, in his intellectual aspect, as a man of high genius, brimful and overflowing with ideas and views . . . He had an intellect as critical and logical as it was speculative and bold . . . It is difficult to enumerate the precise additions to my theological creed which I derived from a friend to whom I owe so much. He made me look with admiration towards the Church of Rome, and in the same degree to dislike the Reformation. He fixed deep in me the idea of devotion to the Blessed Virgin, and he led me gradually to believe in the Real Presence.[3]

In a beautiful sermon Newman preached in 1835 he spoke words that few other Anglicans would have uttered in those days:

> Who can estimate the holiness and perfection of her, who was chosen to be the Mother of Christ? What must have been the angelic purity of her, whom the Creator Spirit condescended to overshadow with His miraculous presence? What must have been her gifts, who was chosen to be the only near earthly relative of the Son of God, the only one whom He was bound by nature to revere and look up to; the one appointed to train and educate Him, to instruct Him day by day, as He grew in wisdom and in stature? For what, think you, was the sanctity and grace of that human nature, of which God formed His sinless Son; knowing,

as we do, 'that which is born of the flesh, is flesh'; and that 'none can bring a clean thing out of an unclean?'[4]

In Oriel College Common Room a movement, later to be known as the Oxford Movement, was stirring. Froude died young in 1836 and Newman lost a dear friend indeed: but he had others. There was Edward Bouverie Pusey, a Fellow of Oriel who soon left Oxford to pursue his studies in Germany, before returning as Regius Professor of Hebrew. And there was John Keble.

Keble's had been the first name Newman had heard mentioned, not just with admiration but with reverence, soon after coming to Oxford. They only overlapped by a year, because Keble went to assist his father, who was a vicar in Fairford, but they were destined to become close friends when he returned to Oxford as Professor of Poetry eight years later. Keble's collection of poetry, *The Christian Year*, published in 1827, contained teaching Newman called 'so deep, so pure, so beautiful' it awoke in him, as it did in the hearts of thousands, a new appreciation of the mystery of the sacraments. Christians everywhere love to sing 'Blest are the Pure in Heart', perhaps the most famous poem in his collection. Keble led Newman to see how the intellectual grasp of truth is taken up by the imagination and heart into faith in the living, personal and present God. It is faith and love that give intellectual probability its certainty. Newman was to take Keble's idea much further in his later sermons and essays, and to its conclusion in *A Grammar of Assent*, published in his seventieth year; offered to show how it is possible to believe what cannot be understood or absolutely proved. It is a theme to which he returned again and again: that doctrine, far from being merely a matter of the intellect, or dealing with abstractions, is the bearer of objective truths, which can be known with certitude and assented to with joy and ease. On this the spiritual life is built. We may hear an echo of Newman in *Dei Verbum* of the Second Vatican Council, which speaks of the Holy Spirit moving the heart and opening the eyes of the mind, 'making it easy for all to accept and believe the truth'.[5]

Vicar of St Mary's

In 1828 Newman, as well as being a tutor at Oriel, was appointed vicar of the University Church, St Mary the Virgin, a prestigious assignment for one so young. The parish included the village of Littlemore that lacked a church. This deficiency Newman soon remedied when his mother, who had come to live nearby, laid the foundation stone of a charming church in 1835. In a few years, Littlemore would become a pivotal centre in his life.

At the University Church, as one of the Select University Preachers, he inaugurated Sunday afternoon sermons at 4:00, and these *Parochial and Plain Sermons*, 600 of them, of which about a third were published and remain in print, were, he acknowledged, the source of his influence among students, graduates, fellows and townspeople who packed the church to hear him over the next fifteen years. He called for conversion and preached often of sanctification, of 'the indwelling of the Holy Trinity within us', or 'the indwelling of Christ', 'the indwelling of the Holy Spirit' or 'the indwelling of Christ in us through the Holy Spirit'. 'He pervades us . . . as a light pervades a building, or as a sweet perfume the folds of some honourable robe; so that in Scripture language, we are said to be in Him, and He in us.' This remained at the heart of his teaching. His words converted and inspired:

> A true Christian, then, may almost be defined as one who has a ruling sense of God's Presence with him. As none but the justified persons have that privilege, so none but the justified have that practical perception of it . . . they only are justified in God's judgment, who give up the notion of justifying themselves by word or deed, who start with the confession that they are unjust, and who come to God, not upon their own merits, but for His mercy . . . In all circumstances, of joy or sorrow, hope or fear, let us aim at having Him in our inmost heart; let us have no secret apart from Him. Let us acknowledge Him as enthroned within us at the very springs of thought and affection . . . this is the true life of saints. This is to have the Spirit witnessing with our spirits that we are sons of God.[6]

> When a man comes to God to be saved, then, I say, the essence of true conversion is a surrender of himself, an unreserved, unconditional surrender . . . What is it that we who profess religion lack? I repeat it, this: a willingness to be changed, a willingness to suffer (if I may use such a word), to suffer Almighty God to change us. We do not like to let go our old selves.[7]

He preached quietly; read his sermons; used no gestures or rhetorical devices: but his words pierced the heart. William Wilberforce said of Newman's preaching that, 'it seemed as if his very soul and body glowed with sternly suppressed emotion'. Matthew Arnold recalled 'the charm of the spiritual apparition, gliding into the dim afternoon light through the aisles of St. Mary's, rising into the pulpit, and then, in the most entrancing of voices, breaking the silence with words and thoughts which were a religious music'. His stillness in the pulpit meant he didn't attract attention to himself. Dean Church, who knew him well and often heard him, described how the sermons 'made men think of the things which the preacher spoke of, and not of the sermon or the preacher'.[8] William Lockhart, a student, said that Newman's sermons had the effect of 'a new revelation. He had the wondrous, the supernatural power of raising the mind to God, and of rooting deeply in us a personal conviction of God, and a sense of His Presence'.[9] Principal Shairp, a Presbyterian Professor of Poetry, said of him:

> The look and bearing of the preacher were as one who dwelt apart, who, though he knew his age well did not dwell in it. From the seclusion of study and abstinence, and prayer, from habitual dwelling in the unseen, he seemed to come forth that one day of the week to speak to others of the things he had seen and known. Or, as others put it, 'He spoke as one who saw'.[10]

His sermons were braced with Christian dogma (doctrines revealed by God), yet nothing was dry: he made them so relevant to his congregation. What impressed Anthony Froude the historian, and brother of Hurrell, was the way he understood the needs of his hearers:

> No one who heard his sermons in those days can ever forget them. They were seldom theological. We had theology enough and to spare from the Select Preachers of the university. Newman, taking some Scripture character for a text, spoke to us about ourselves, our temptations, our experiences. His illustrations were inexhaustible. He seemed to be addressing the most secret consciousness of each of us ... A sermon from him was a poem formed by a single idea ... fascinating by its subtlety, welcome—how welcome!—from its sincerity, interesting from its originality even to those who were careless of religion; and to others who wished to be religious, but had found religion dry and wearisome, it was like the springing of a fountain out of the rock'.[11]

He went on to describe a sermon in which Newman recounted closely some incidents in Our Lord's Passion:

> And then he paused. For a few moments there was a breathless silence. Then in a low clear voice, of which the faintest vibration was audible in the farthest corner of St Mary's, he said, 'Now I bid you consider that He to whom these things were done was Almighty God'. It was as if an electric stroke was gone through the church. As if every person present understood for the first time the meaning of what he had all his life been saying.[12]

Newman had his Evangelical critics who thought that because his demands were severe, he must necessarily be neglecting to preach on the free gift of God's grace. Newman was unapologetic. He was preaching in a Church that, to him, had become lax and where even many of the clergy led a complacent, comfortable life. God's love and his grace summon us to be saints, to bear hardships for the sake of the Gospel. Catholics were not used to such preaching either, and after he became a Catholic, his Bishop, William Ullathorne, worried lest his standards would be too high for ordinary people.[13]

The reality is that he spoke of God who, while calling us to holiness, is all-loving:

> It is then the duty and privilege of all disciples of our glorified Saviour, to be exalted and transfigured with Him; to live in heaven in their thoughts, motives, aims, desires, likings, prayers, praises, intercessions, even while they are in the flesh; to look like other men, to be busy like other men, to be passed over in the crowd of men or even to be scorned or oppressed, as other men may be, but the while to have a secret channel of communication with the Most High, a gift the world knows not of; to have their life hid with Christ in God.[14]

It was the vogue in Newman's day for sermons to be printed, and Newman observed that he thought his influence 'among persons who have not seen me has been indefinitely greater than those who have'. Prime Minister William Gladstone was asked 'which of Newman's writings will be read in a hundred years'? I think all his parochial sermon will be read', he replied.[15] And so it proved. His sermons have run into multiple editions, and are as popular as ever today.

As well as his Parochial and Plain Sermons he also preached fifteen Sermons before the University of Oxford between 1826 and 1843, as part of his duties as a 'Select Preacher'. Another twenty-six were collected under the title *Sermons bearing upon Subjects of the Day* because 'they are to be read and understood mainly with reference to their . . . bearing on the occasion and circumstances of their first publication'. In *The Apostolical Christian* Newman reminds his people that one of the graces of New Testament Christianity

> is not only a pure heart, not only a clean hand, but thirdly a cheerful countenance. I say joy in all its forms, for in true joyfulness many graces are included; joyful people are loving; joyful people are forgiving; joyful people are munificent. Joy, if it be Christian joy, the refined joy of the mortified and persecuted, makes men peaceful, serene, thankful, gentle, affectionate, sweet-tempered, pleasant, hopeful; it is graceful, tender, touching, winning. All this were the Christians of the New Testament, for they had obtained what they desired. They had desired to sacrifice the kingdom of the world and all its pomps for the love of Christ.[16]

This collection on *Subjects of the Day* completes the corpus of his Anglican sermons, and includes his final one preached in Littlemore Church,

'The Parting of Friends'.

As well as introducing his Sunday afternoon sermons, Newman changed the liturgies in St Mary's. He began to say Morning Prayer publicly in church in 1834, and from 1837 a daily early Holy Communion Service. He was recalling the Church of England back to its Catholic roots, and these practices spread all over England and the Empire too.

Not everyone was happy. The influence of Newman on students was so compelling that the head of Wadham College resented him and organised compulsory lectures on Sunday afternoons in an attempt to prevent his undergraduates from attending St Mary's. One of Newman's lasting legacies to university teaching is the now commonplace tutorial system, which he introduced with Hurrell Froude and Robert Wilberforce (the son of William Wilberforce). College tutors did little more than lecture, and the more serious students would hire private tutors at some expense, if they could afford them. Newman and his friends argued, from their understanding of education, and also from earlier custom at Oxford, that tutors should offer free tutorials as part of their normal teaching method, creating a meeting of minds with their students, and an academic and a pastoral relationship with them. However, the newly appointed Provost of Oriel, Edward Hawkins, whom Newman had succeeded as vicar of St Mary's, and from whom Newman confessed he had learned much about the catholic side of Anglicanism, strongly disagreed with Newman's radical revision of the tutorial system, and in 1830 informed Newman that no further students would be sent to him.

It was almost the end of his illustrious academic career at Oxford (though he remained vicar of St Mary's): at the time very shocking, on another level it marked the beginning of a new life. Much later, in 1864, in his *Apologia pro Vita Sua* the 'history of my religious opinions', Newman describes a turning point in his brilliantly successful life as a young Oxford don when he realised that he 'was beginning to prefer intellectual excellence to moral; I was drifting in the direction of the Liberalism of the day'. Newman recognised that God often uses disappointments for his own purposes and so it proved to be for Newman. On leaving Oriel, free from teaching duties, Newman was able to accept a commission to write a book on the history of the Church Councils which ended up as *The Arians of the Fourth Century.*

His former students showed their gratitude and appreciation by presenting him with volumes of the Fathers; those Christian theologians (some contemporary with New Testament writers and others who followed them), with whose help, Newman had come to believe, the New Testament should be interpreted for its earliest, apostolic meaning. This way of discovering Christian doctrine in the New Testament differed sharply from that of the Evangelicals who treated the Bible as if it was a source book of texts to be interpreted without regard for the history and life of the Church in which it was inspired and written. Like many of the other Oxford Movement leaders, especially Dr Pusey, the chief editor of the Library of the Fathers, Newman became an authority on the Fathers. In years to come he reflected:

> In truth, this fidelity of the ancient Christian system, seen in modern Rome, was the luminous fact which more than any other turned men's minds at Oxford forty years ago to look towards her with reverence, interest and love. It affected individual minds variously of course: some it eventually brought on to conversion, others it only restrained from active opposition to her claims; but none of us could read the Fathers, and determine to be their disciples, without feeling that Rome, like a faithful steward, had kept in fullness and vigour what our own communion had let drop.[17]

One of the most charming books Newman wrote was a novel, *Callista*. Composed in his mellifluous style and meticulously researched, it tells the story of the Christian Church in North Africa; vividly picturing its life, to show what early Christianity was really like during the third century, in the days of the Fathers. It was written in 1855, but that is to leap ahead.

After the stresses of the previous few years, in 1832 Newman was easily persuaded by Hurrell Froude and his father to join them on a holiday in the Mediterranean. They visited Rome and attended Mass offered by Pope Gregory XVI on the feast of the Annunciation in the Church of Santa Maria sopra Minerva: the first Catholic Mass Newman had attended. He was not impressed by the pomp and show, the luxurious altar dressings and vestments, the appearance of the Sovereign Pontiff and of the religious 'court of Rome' with its sumptuously dressed cardinals.

Twice he met Monsignor Nicholas Wiseman, the Rector of the English College. He also met the Dean of Malta, but otherwise 'kept clear of Catholics throughout our tour'. When the Froude's returned home Newman went on to Sicily where he fell seriously ill, possibly of typhoid. It seemed he might die, yet he was certain he would live 'for God has still some work for me to do'. For want of a ship he was forced to spend three weeks in Palermo. Aching to get home, he found calmness in visiting churches, though did not go to Mass or any services. Then, on an orange boat bound for Marseilles, he was becalmed for a week in the Strait of Bonifacio, where he wrote his moving poem 'Lead Kindly Light', which became a much-loved hymn. It expressed so well Newman's desire to trust in God's guidance and presence, to let not pride rule his will, and his contentment to let God show him the way, 'one step enough for me'.

During the holiday Newman had been disturbed by news from England about interference in the Anglican Church by the Government, with its Irish Church Reform Bill to suppress ten bishoprics in Ireland. He reached England on 10 July 1833, and the following Sunday in St Mary's Church heard John Keble preach a rejoinder to the Bill before the Judges of Assize in a sermon entitled 'National Apostasy', calling on the State and its leaders to return to God from their apostasy, and to respect the Church and its bishops who are the successors of the apostles. The sensation caused by the sermon convinced these Oxford friends of the influence they could have if they tried. Years of discussions in Oriel College were coming to fruition. Keble's sermon, Newman maintained, was when the Oxford Movement began, though in truth it had been gestating for several years.

3

The Oxford Movement

TEN DAYS after the Assize Sermon, Hugh James Rose, Professor of Divinity at the recently founded Durham University, hosted a meeting in his rectory at Hadleigh in Essex. Keble and Newman were not present but Hurrell Froude was; along with William Palmer, a deacon who constructed what became known as the 'Branch Theory', and Arthur Perceval, the rector of East Horsley. They agreed that a series of Tracts for the Times should be written to address issues raised by the Sermon. It gave the Oxford Movement its first name, *Tractarianism*.

Tracts for The Times

First off the press in September 1833, was a four-page penny Tract by Newman on the Apostolic Succession entitled *Thoughts on the Ministerial Commission, respectfully addressed to the Clergy*. It contained a passionate call for bishops (especially), as well as priests and deacons to live up to their calling: 'act up to your professions. Let it not be said that you have neglected a gift; for if you have the Spirit of the Apostles on you, surely this is a great gift. "Stir up the gift of God which is in you". Make much of it. Show your value of it.' Recalling that bishops 'stand the brunt of the battle' . . . and that upon them comes 'the care of all the Churches . . . indeed it is their glory', Newman declared 'Not one of us would wish in the least to deprive them of the duties, the toils, the responsibilities of their high Office. And, black event as it would be for the country, yet, (as far as they are concerned,) we could not wish them a more blessed termination of their course, than the spoiling of their goods, and martyrdom'. 'We encroach not upon the rights of the SUCCESSORS OF THE APOSTLES [*sic*]; we touch not their sword and crosier. Yet surely we may be their shield-bearers in the battle without offence'.

Newman and the Tractarians were determined to proclaim that the Church of England, far from being a department of State as many saw it, is a divine institution founded by Christ himself. Its authority was not given to it by the State but has been handed down from generation

15

to generation to the present-day bishops from the apostles, whose successors they are, though they scarcely realised it, or lived like it.

Within a year, forty-seven anonymous *Tracts* had been published, mostly written by Newman; with others by Keble, Froude and a layman, John Bowden. One of them, on fasting, was written by Pusey, which he boldly signed with his initials to signify his formal adhesion to the Movement. Around and about Oxford, from parsonage to parsonage, rode Newman and his friends on horseback distributing bundles of *Tracts*, which were eagerly sought and bought. The pamphlets spread far. Meetings assembled to discuss them: gatherings, dinners, soirées and a voluminous correspondence ensued, Newman reinforcing it all by packing St Mary's with his brilliant *Parochial Sermons*.

Despite the fact that some *Tracts* contained attacks on Rome (like Tract 20 'their Communion is infected with heresy: we are bound to flee it as a pestilence'), the pamphlets were denounced as 'popery'. What they sought to do and in many ways succeeded in doing, was to recall the Church of England to its past, and revive a deeper understanding of the nature of the Church: its worship, its discipline, and its catholic and apostolic origins.

To appreciate the enormous impact of the *Tracts*, it is necessary to know something about the state of the Church of England in those days. More than half the clergy resided outside their parishes in 'better parts'. Families sent their sons 'into the Church' to be ordained because it was expected. With few exceptions bishops were indolent and wealthy, hardly ever visiting their parishes or administering Confirmation. The Bishop of Winchester, for example, was said to have an income of £50,000 a year, while curates were paid £60 a year or less by incumbents made rich through holding livings in plurality. One Bishop of Llandaff hardly ever set foot in the diocese he ruled for over twenty years, proudly spending his time as an agriculturalist and bringing up his family in the purer air of the Lake District. A Bishop of Bristol had his palace burned down by a mob in 1831. Nor are these isolated instances, for although there certainly were some devout and industrious clergy, particularly among the Evangelicals, the abuses of pluralism, non-residence, nepotism, simony and sinecures had flourished almost without interruption since before the Reformation. An act against pluralism passed in the reign of Henry VIII had been completely ineffective. The Catholic Church on the continent had confronted the same abuses by means of the Council of Trent (1545–63) with marked success and a flood of missionary enterprise. Seminaries were established to educate the clergy and inspire their sense of vocation. But the Church of England had to wait three centuries for the Oxford Movement to achieve similar reforms.

With such pastors the Church of England was inevitably in poor shape. Some cathedrals were nearly in ruins and it was even proposed by one speaker at a public meeting that Canterbury Cathedral should be given over to the local cavalry for stables. Some parish churches were well-attended, especially in the towns, but Holy Communion was celebrated no more than four or five times a year. The sick could not be anointed and confession had disappeared. Services were dreary and strangers to joy, though the singing of hymns was becoming popular among Evangelicals.

The Reformation had abolished religious communities, and the country never properly recovered from the loss of health and social care they provided. Pew rents effectively kept away poor people who, if they wanted to worship somewhere, were drawn to the non-conformist chapels. Until Newman and his friends began to preach about holiness and service, and inspire people to lead converted lives, only Evangelicals and non-conformists were making serious efforts to do so. (The Catholic Church in Britain had been virtually destroyed by the Reformation.) Concern about the state of the Church of England was widespread. The headmaster of Rugby School, Thomas Arnold, wrote in 1832 'The Church as it now stands no human power can save'.[1] He spoke more truly than he knew. A year later God raised up the *Movement*, as Newman called it.

The *Tracts for the Times* fell like sparks on the dry tinder of the Church. They had to be reprinted to meet demand. Their effect was tremendous and the support was astonishing. So was the opposition. Criticism of them reached fever pitch in 1841 when the ninetieth tract was published. Here, following the line of a seventeenth-century Catholic Franciscan priest, Christopher Davenport, it was argued that the Thirty-Nine Articles of the Church of England are not contrary to Roman Catholic doctrine. They were aimed at corrupt practices rather than doctrine, and are consequently capable of a Catholic interpretation. Hoping thereby to stem the tide of Anglicans already beginning to 'go over to Rome' the tract argued that all things necessary could be found within the Church of England, including seven sacraments, the Real Presence of the Eucharist, a proper doctrine of purgatory, and the invocation of saints.

The whole body of Protestant England rose up in fury against *Tract 90*. No one doubted that Newman was its author, though in truth Keble had pressed him to publish it. A violent torrent of abuse was hurled at Newman. The heads of the Oxford colleges raged in opposition, declaring the tract incompatible with the university statutes, and accusing Newman of being a dishonest man. The Bishop of Oxford banned the publication of further tracts: Newman's life in Oxford was ended.

The effect on him was catastrophic and appalling. 'In every part of the country and every class of society, in newspapers, in pulpits, at dinner-tables, in coffee-rooms, in railway carriages, I was denounced as a traitor'. Needing to consider his future, and virtually driven from the Church of England by public opinion and hostile bishops, he and a small community of followers slipped into exile at Littlemore, where he had leased a few cottages. These cottages are now occupied by Sisters of the Society of the Work, who will show you his study, left almost the same as when he lived, worked and prayed there. In September 1843 he resigned his living of St Mary's, and preached in Littlemore Church his last sermon as vicar, which he called 'The Parting of Friends'. He ended with this emotional call:

> And, O my brethren, O kind and affectionate hearts, O loving friends, should you know anyone whose lot it has been, by writing or by word of mouth, in some degree to help you thus to act; if he has ever told you what you knew about yourselves, or what you did not know; has read to you your wants or feelings, and comforted you by the very reading; has made you feel that there was a higher life than this daily one, and a brighter world than that you see; or encouraged you, or sobered you, or opened a way to the inquiring, or soothed the perplexed; if what he has said or done has ever made you take interest in him, and feel well inclined towards him; remember such a one in time to come, though you hear him not, and pray for him, that in all things he may know God's will, and at all times he may be ready to fulfil it.[2]

A few days later he celebrated Holy Communion for the last time, in St Mary's, with Dr Pusey.

Newman at Littlemore

It is clear that at this time he did not 'know God's will' for himself. Yet even before *Tract 90* was published a doubt had entered his mind, as he revealed to Bishop Wiseman to whom he dedicated his first book of Catholic sermons in 1849. 'I cannot forget that when, in the year 1839, a doubt first crossed my mind of the tenableness of the theological theory on which Anglicanism is based, it was caused in no slight degree by the perusal of a controversial paper, attributed to your Lordship, on the schism of the Donatists'.[3]

He continued to live with his community at Littlemore, spending four and a half hours each day in prayer: nine more in translating the treatises of St Athanasius against Arius. What was he to do? He was being drawn to the Catholic Church, yet he was ignorant of it. He knew more about the Catholic Church in its early centuries than the actual Church of his own day. 'I had once been into Warwick Street Chapel, with my father, who, I believe, wanted to hear some piece of music'. He recalls in his *Apologia*, 'all that I bore away from it was the recollection of a pulpit and a preacher, and a boy swinging a censer'. True, Newman had encountered Catholicism briefly in Rome on his Mediterranean tour, where he met and admired some Catholic priests. Other than attending Mass offered by Pope Gregory XVI, as mentioned, he chose not to go to Mass. He disagreed with the Church's teachings on purgatory, indulgences, the invocation of saints, and the pope.

What was he to do? He could not become a Catholic when he didn't believe these fundamental dogmas taught by the Church. For more than four years at Littlemore Newman struggled with his intellectual problem of thinking that Roman Catholics had added to the truths revealed in Scripture. Man of integrity as he was, he could not take one step towards the Catholic Church with this massive difficulty unresolved. He began to write what he called an 'Essay on the Development of Doctrine'. Just as all great human ideas develop over time, so, in a sense, he realised, does the understanding of Christian doctrines develop:

> time is necessary for the full comprehension and perfection of great ideas; and that the highest and most wonderful truths, though communicated to the world once for all by inspired teachers, could not be comprehended all at once by the recipients, but, as being received and transmitted by minds not inspired and through media which were human, have required only the longer time and deeper thought for their full elucidation. This may be called the Theory of Development of Doctrine.[4]

Gradually the clouds began to disperse: light dawned. Development belongs to the very nature of the Church, its Gospel and its doctrine:

> If Christianity be an universal religion, suited not simply to one locality or period, but to all times and places, it cannot but vary in its relations and dealings towards the world around it, that is, it will develop.[5]

It is plain that fundamental doctrines like the Holy Trinity and the Incarnation of Christ had developed from Scripture, becoming more explicit and articulated in the fourth century. Similarly, doctrines about papal supremacy, the Mother of God and purgatory are not additions to the Gospel, as he had thought, but are the outcome of the Church's pondering upon the Gospel; just as in one sense the New Testament books themselves are from the words of Jesus. There is no new revelation, but teachings naturally develop. What was implicit at the beginning becomes explicit. Christian dogma grows, rather than accumulates, in a 'continuous tradition from the earliest time'. Revealed doctrine received and transmitted through the minds of many generations of theologians and councils develops, and this requires the Church to be able to distinguish true developments from false. He delineated seven tests (he later called them 'notes') to ascertain whether particular developments are in continuity with tradition or not, and concluded that this requires an infallible and living authority.

> The common sense of mankind ... feels that the very idea of revelation implies a present informant and guide, and that an infallible one ... We are told that God has spoken. Where? In a book? We have tried it and it disappoints; it disappoints us, that holy and most blessed gift, not from any fault of its own, but because it is used for a purpose for which it was not given. The Ethiopian's reply, when St Philip asked him if he understood what he was reading, is the voice of nature; 'How can I, unless someone shall guide me?' The Church undertakes that office.[6]

He elucidated further:

> Revelation is a heavenly gift. He who gave it virtually has not given it, unless He has also secured it from perversion and corruption, in all such development as comes upon it by the necessity of its nature, or, in other words, that that intellectual action through successive generations, which is the organ of development, must, so far forth as it can claim to have been put in charge of the revelation, be in its determinations infallible.[7]

Such an infallible authority exists, he realised; and has always existed. The Fathers, to whom Newman continually appealed, had been the very ones who witnessed to this authority, the authority of the Church itself and in particular the authority of the bishop of Rome, the pope, the successor of St Peter. The Roman Catholic Church of the nineteenth century was by no means the same in every respect as the Church of early centuries, any more than the man is the same as the boy, but it was clearly the same body, the same living community, continuously developing in history.

This threw a sledgehammer into the Branch Theory by which Tractarians had maintained that the Church of England is a part or a 'branch' of the Catholic Church. They taught that the Catholic Church had become divided into three branches, Roman, Orthodox and Anglican. For Newman now, the Church had no branches. All antiquity bore witness to the unity of the Church. There could be no such thing as a 'branch' of the Catholic Church, so the Church of England was not part of the Catholic Church but in schism from it. 'Men of Catholic views are too truly but a party in our Church'. Utilising his study of the Arians he argued that Protestants were in a position similar to the Arians, while the *via media* of Anglicanism resembled the situation of the semi-Arians.

He concluded that the question of development turned on the nature of the promise of the Holy Spirit and the unity of the Church. While he was writing his *Essay* he wrote letters to unnamed friends, which reveal the way his mind was moving.

> I must tell you then frankly ... that it is not from disappointment, irritation, or impatience, that I have, whether rightly or wrongly, resigned St Mary's; but because I think the Church of Rome the Catholic Church, and ours not part of the Catholic Church, because not in communion with Rome; and because I feel that I could not honestly be a teacher in it any longer.[8]

To another he wrote:

> And as far as I know myself, my one paramount reason for contemplating a change is my deep, unvarying conviction that our church is in schism, and that my salvation depends on my joining the Church of Rome.[9]

In a letter to a Visitation nun he explained:

> At present, my full belief is ... that, if there is a move in our Church, very few persons indeed will be partners to it. I doubt whether one or two at the most among residents at Oxford. And I don't know whether I can wish it. The state of the Roman Catholics is at present so unsatisfactory. This I am sure of, that nothing but a simple, direct call of duty is a warrant for any one leaving our Church; no preference of another Church, no delight in its services, no hope of greater religious advancement in it, no indignation, no disgust, at the persons and things, among which we may find ourselves in the Church of England. The simple question is, Can *I* (it is personal, not whether another, but can *I*) be saved in the English Church? Am *I* in safety, were I to die tonight? Is it a mortal sin in *me*, not joining another communion?[10]

The state of the Roman Catholics was indeed unsatisfactory, as he said. What had been the glorious medieval Catholic Church in England no longer existed. Its place had been usurped by the Anglican Church. There were few Catholics in England when Newman was born: only about 30,000 in the whole country, drawn mainly from old 'recusant' families who had kept the Faith since the Reformation and refused at huge cost and suffering to be Anglican; together with French Catholics who had fled the Revolution, settled in England and made some converts here. There were no catholic churches, no parishes: no dioceses only 'Districts', nothing you could call the 'Catholic Church'. But in 1850 Pope Pius IX recognised the need to restore a normal hierarchy of bishops and dioceses. To celebrate this momentous event, Newman was invited to preach at the First Provincial Synod of Westminster at St Mary's Oscott in 1852. In a moving sermon entitled 'The Second Spring': so moving that Nicholas Wiseman, by then Cardinal Archbishop of Westminster, and many more; were in tears. Newman described what it was like to be a Catholic in early nineteenth century England:

> No longer the Catholic Church in the country; nay, no longer, I may say, a Catholic community—but a few adherents of the Old Religion, moving silently and sorrowfully about, as memorials of what had been. 'The Roman Catholics'—not a sect, not even an interest, as men conceived of it—not a body, however small, representative of the Great Communion abroad—but a mere handful of individuals, who might be counted, like the pebbles and detritus of the great deluge, and who, forsooth, merely happened to retain a creed which, in its day indeed, was the profession of a Church. Here a set of poor Irishmen, coming and going at harvest time, or a colony of them lodged in a miserable quarter of the vast metropolis. There, perhaps an elderly person, seen walking in the streets, grave and solitary, and strange, though noble in bearing, and said to be of good family, and a 'Roman Catholic' . . . who they were, or what they did, or what was meant by calling them Roman Catholics, no one could tell—though it had an unpleasant sound, and told of form and superstition. And then, perhaps, as we went to and fro, looking with a boy's curious eyes through the great city, we might come . . . on a chapel of the 'Roman Catholics': but nothing was to be gathered from it, except that there were lights burning there, and some boys in white, swinging censers; and what it all meant could only be learned from books, from Protestant Histories and Sermons; and they did not report well of 'the Roman Catholics', but, on the contrary, deposed that they had once had power and had abused it.[11]

Before all this, at Littlemore, now no longer vicar of St Mary's, Newman was wrestling with his conscience and his intellect, and writing his 'Essay on the Development of Doctrine'. Before the essay was finished Newman knew what he must do. 'As I advanced, my view so cleared that instead of speaking any more of "the Roman Catholics", I boldly called them Catholics. Before I got to the end, I resolved to be received, and the book remains in the state in which it was then, unfinished'. In fact he stopped writing mid-sentence. On 3 October 1845 he wrote to the Provost of Oriel resigning his Fellowship. On 9 October, after writing a few letters to his sister and friends, Oxford's greatest son, the light of his generation, humbly asked an Italian Passionist priest, a distinguished philosopher, Fr Dominic Barberi (now Blessed Dominic) to hear his confession and receive him into what he had come to believe to be 'the one and only fold of the Redeemer'.

— 4 —

The Double Legacy
of the Oxford Movement

NEWMAN NEVER DOUBTED for a moment that the Oxford Movement was raised up by God. After becoming a Catholic he wrote: 'Providence does nothing in vain; so much earnestness, zeal, toil, thought, religiousness, success, as has a place in the history of that Movement, must surely have a place also in His scheme'.[1] But what is that place? At the start of it, Newman and his associates were seeking to renew the Church of England, emancipate it from State control, and reconnect it with its Catholic roots. Then perforce Newman changed his opinion. He believed that in God's providence the purpose of the Movement was to lead its members into the Catholic Church as it had him and those who followed him; and indeed as it has continued to do, not least when some crisis has arisen in the Anglican Church that they felt undermined their position. This in no way denies that the original purpose of the Movement was the renewal of the Church of England: but it found this other purpose too. We can properly speak of the double legacy of the Oxford Movement.

Although hundreds of Anglicans, mainly Oxford and Cambridge intellectuals and their families, followed Newman over the next few years, the great majority in the Oxford Movement held true to the original idea; remaining in the Church of England to continue its renewal. How Pusey, on whom now fell the mantle of leading the Oxford Movement, held it together is a remarkable story. Newman faced a barrage of criticism at abandoning the Movement, but Pusey never joined in. Late in the evening of Newman's last day in Oxford he came to say goodbye, and he wrote most kindly of him in a letter to the *English Churchman*:

> Our Church has not known how to employ him. And since this was so, it seemed as if a sharp sword were lying in its scabbard ... He seems to me not so much gone from us, as transplanted into another part of the vineyard, where the full energies of his powerful mind can be employed.

He went on:

> It is perhaps the greatest event which has happened since the communion of the Churches has been interrupted, that such an one, so formed in our Church, and the work of God's Spirit as dwelling within her, should be transplanted to theirs. If anything could open their eyes to what is good in us, or soften in us any wrong prejudices against them, it would be the presence of such an one, nurtured and grown to such ripeness in our Church, and now removed to theirs.[2]

As the nineteenth century progressed the effect of the Movement on the Church of England became profound. Renewal began as Newman perceived it must, with the clergy. The abuses of pluralism, non-residence, nepotism and simony were tackled, and as the century proceeded the clergymen caricatured or highlighted by Jane Austen, were succeeded by bishops and priests of sincere conviction. Newman's first Tract had sought to rouse the clergy from their quiet worldliness. In due course many chose to be celibate, and some became affectionately known as 'slum priests' because they devoted themselves to serving people in the most deprived parishes of countryside and cities. Thomas Keble, the younger brother of John (and an author of four of the *Tracts*) had been the first to do this, when in 1827 he became vicar of Bisley, a sprawling parish mainly inhabited by very poor and neglected agricultural labourers and weavers. Some priests founded communities of Sisters, a revival of the religious life, to assist and nurse the poor. Their joyful self-sacrificing lives were beautifully described in the memoirs of Jennifer Worth, who worked with the Community of St John the Divine in the East End of London. It led to the very popular television series *Call the Midwife*.

Religious orders for men were also established, including contemplative communities. Small theological colleges were set up beside cathedrals, offering students a good intellectual preparation and a semi-monastic priestly formation. Religious communities like the Community of the Resurrection, Mirfield and the Society of the Sacred Mission, Kelham also undertook the training of priests. The Benedictine Abbey of Nashdom produced the brilliant liturgical scholar, Dom Gregory Dix, OSB, and pioneered ecumenism. Other scholars made a mark on biblical and theological studies, and still do. Good priests raised the spiritual life of the Church of England, and more of its Catholic heritage was recovered. Religious communities and missionary societies took the Gospel to Africa, India and other developing countries, and many of them still work there today. Mirfield Fathers, notably Fr Trevor Huddleston, CR, played a heroic part in helping combat apartheid in South Africa. Anglican Sisters are still found in some of the most fearful countries of the world, like the Sisters of the Society of St Margaret in Haiti.

The Movement grew with the years and the Church of England was transformed. Not just Sunday, but daily Eucharists were established. The word 'Mass' became commonly used (especially as in 'Midnight Mass' at Christmas), and the practice of retreats and classical ways of prayer were revived. Devotion to the Blessed Virgin Mary and the saints was fostered. In 1922 the Shrine of Our Lady of Walsingham was restored, and in due course other shrines too, that had been destroyed in the reign of Henry VIII; a tangible legacy of the Oxford Movement. All seven sacraments including confession came back. Parish confraternities and guilds for lay people to encourage their spiritual lives, along with manuals of prayer and meditation, spiritual reading and Bible-reading aids continue to be a mark of the 'Catholic Movement', as it came to be called. The Movement produced some notable hymn-writers, as well as translators of ancient Greek, Latin, and medieval hymns, and their work is to be found not only in Anglican but in Catholic hymnals and in the English edition of the Divine Office too. Some of these writers became Catholics, others remained Anglican. Where would we be without hymns like 'O come, all ye faithful'; 'All glory, laud, and honour'; and 'At the Cross her station keeping'?

Newman kept in touch with the Movement through those who remained his friends, and when Anglo-Catholic (as they came to be called) priests suffered imprisonment under the Public Worship Regulation Act of 1874 for the crimes of wearing eucharistic vestments and putting candles on the altar (which are now commonplace), Newman observed, with his ironic humour, that he could only 'heartily wish a good number . . . may get into prison' to show up their liberal opponents as 'flagrant persecutors'.

Newman was nonetheless anxious about those who rejected, as he did, the Branch Theory, yet for various 'difficulties' remained outside the Catholic Church. In 1850 he gave a series of lectures which were published as *Difficulties of Anglicans*. What made him deliver the lectures was 'my intimate sense that the Catholic Church is the one ark of salvation, and my love for your souls'.[3] He emphasised his teaching on conscience, and why people must follow their conscience, whatever the cost. It is a matter of salvation. He knew that his secession had caused pain to many: harsh criticism had come his way, but he reminded them that he would not have left the English Church had he thought it possible to stay in God's favour and remain. He joined the Catholic Church, he told them, 'simply because he believed it, and it only, to be the Church of the Fathers; because he believed that there was a Church upon earth till the end of time, and one only ... did St. Athanasius or St Ambrose come suddenly to life it cannot be doubted what communion they would recognise, for their own.'[4]

He pleaded with high churchmen who thought they should remain Anglican to help make it more Catholic. It would not happen. It is an Established National Church and nothing could make it Catholic. 'You can have no trust in the Establishment or its Sacraments and ordinances. You must leave it, you must secede ... You must take up your cross, and you must go hence'.[5]

This, however, was not his last word on the subject. Unlike other zealous converts, Newman never tried to press individuals to join him. Indeed he thought it 'highly injudicious, indiscreet, wanton, to interfere with them in particular cases'.[6] He recognised them to be on the same side as Catholics 'in this evil day of scepticism and infidelity'. In 1850 he warned a layman, J. M. Capes, who wanted to launch a crusade against the Establishment of the Church of England, that it is a 'bulwark against infidelity ... *till* the Catholic Church is strong enough to take its place'.[7] In 1863, speaking of Pusey and his Oxford friends he said 'I feel for them very much now, facing, as they do, so terrible a billow of anxiety and scepticism in faith'. In the same year, to Isaac Williams he reiterated that 'Everything I hear makes me fear that latitudinarian opinions are spreading furiously in the Church of England. I grieve most deeply at it—the Anglican Church has been a most useful breakwater against scepticism'.[8]

In 1857 Ambrose Phillipps de Lisle, a wealthy layman, began a long correspondence with Newman. He had become a Catholic in 1823 (and gave the land on which was built Mount St Bernard Abbey, the first monastery established in England since the Reformation). For a long time he had entertained the hope that the Oxford Movement was going to be a step towards reconciling the Anglican Church to Rome, and he sent Newman a pamphlet he had written suggesting individuals should remain in the Church of England until they could join the Catholic Church in a body. Newman replied that

> There is such an extreme difficulty in rousing the mind to the real *necessity* of leaving the position into which men have grown up, their professions perhaps, their neighbourhood, or their family, or their work, that they will easily avail themselves of any the slightest excuse—and even a hint from a person so deeply respected as yourself, so beloved, yourself too a convert, is more than sufficient to turn the scale, when the mind is in suspense. And then suppose, if these very dear and precious souls, say Dr Pusey, are taken away in this state, when grace has been offered them, and they have not followed it up.[9]

To a correspondent in 1871, who suggested that some Anglo-Catholics were in bad faith, wilfully shutting their eyes upon light which would lead them into the Catholic Church, Newman reminds him 'we must look to ourselves not to others', but in a slightly different vein went on:

> Surely there is another supposable reason for God's dealings with them. They are kept where they are, with no more light than they have, being Anglicans in good faith gradually to prepare their hearers and readers in greater numbers than otherwise would be possible for the true and perfect faith and to lead them on in due season to the Catholic Church ... were they all themselves to fulfil their duty to become Catholics at once now, the work of conversion would simply come to an end.[10]

In 1857 de Lisle and his Catholic and Anglican friends started The Association for the Promotion of the Unity of Christendom to pray and work for corporate reunion between the Catholic, Anglican and Orthodox Churches. Within seven years it claimed 8,000 members of whom 1000 were Catholics, 300 Orthodox and the rest Anglican.[11] de Lisle had an audience with Pope Pius IX in which the Holy Father gave his Blessing to the Association, expressing his delight and amazement that at such an institution had been established with the Church of England. However, Cardinal Wiseman withdrew his initial support and expressed his misgivings to the Holy Office in Rome, which, without actually forbidding Catholics from being members, urged the English bishops to discourage them. His successor, Henry Manning issued in 1866 a stern warning against the Association and listed its theological deficiencies, in particular its advocacy of the Branch Theory that Newman had heartily rejected and is contrary to Catholic teaching. A few months later, in a long, kindly, but firmly discouraging letter to de Lisle, Newman set out 'all I have to say about Corporate Reunion', concluding that such a reunion would take a 'miracle—in the same sense in which it would be a miracle for the Thames to change its course and run into the sea at the Wash'.

The Association survived the setbacks. In 1868 it claimed a membership of 1,881 Catholics and 10,026 Anglicans, and it persisted until the end of the century. Then in due course a new Anglican society, The Catholic League was formed to pray and work for corporate reunion. These pioneering Anglican ecumenists also founded in 1908 the Octave of Prayer for Christian Unity, which under the influence of the French Abbé de Couturier came to be observed, as it still is, as the Week of Prayer for Christian Unity by most Christians throughout the world. It is often said that the Ecumenical Movement began with a gathering of Protestants and Anglicans at the World Missionary Conference of 1910.

It would be more accurate to date it back to 1857, to de Lisle and The Association for the Promotion of the Unity of Christendom.

The idea of corporate reunion actually had a long history before de Lisle. In 1634 Pope Urban VIII, with the approval of King Charles I, sent an agent, Dom Leander, a close friend of Archbishop Laud of Canterbury, with whom he shared rooms at Oxford, to report back on the state of Catholic affairs in England. Following his report the Pope then sent a second agent, Gregory Panzani. He spent two years in England meeting people prominent in Church and State including Archbishop Laud, who recorded in his diary that he was offered a cardinal's hat.[12] Only three Anglican bishops were 'violently against the See of Rome', Panzani reported; and he recommended that Rome should allow married priests, an English liturgy and Communion under both kinds, and permit Catholics to take the Oath of Allegiance to the monarch.[13] Opposition in Parliament, which led to the King's execution and to the Civil War, put an end to it. Archbishop Laud paid dearly for his involvement too; beheaded for 'corresponding with Rome' and 'treating with the Pope's men in England'. After the Civil War ended and the monarchy was restored, the scheme was picked up again in 1663. It included further details: the Archbishop of Canterbury would be designated a patriarch; a provincial synod would be set up; existing bishops and priests could remain in office after re-ordination; certain religious orders were to be restored; and religious freedom granted to Protestants.[14] But, as before, opposition in the country blocked it. Newman knew of this plan, and a later one involving Archbishop Wake of Canterbury; he refers to them in a *Letter to Dr Pusey*.[15]

When, in 1876 de Lisle came up with a similar plan (said to have the backing of Cardinal Manning, the Archbishop of Westminster), he told Newman about it. Newman replied 'nothing will rejoice me more than to find that the Holy See considers it safe and promising to sanction some such plan'. He was sympathetic to any 'means of drawing to us so many good people, who are now shivering at our gates'. Mentioning in particular two married clergy converts in a letter to Mrs William Froude, he thought it was grievous that such men of experience were 'cast out as useless into idleness and hopeless obscurity . . . I cannot help longing for some plan'.[16] But he thought that Rome would not hear of it unless 'the measure was sure to recover half England to the Church'.[17] Yet he reminded de Lisle that Church history showed it was often the case that 'a thing is in itself good, but the time has not come for it . . . I can quite believe that the conversion of Anglicans may be more thorough and more extended, if it is delayed — and our Lord knows more than we do'.[18]

Newman proved prophetic, and the time did come. His hopes that married convert clergy might no longer be 'cast out as useless' was realised in the 1950s when Pope Pius XII granted permission for five married former Lutheran pastors in Germany and some Anglican priests in Australia to be ordained as diocesan Catholic priests. Pope St Paul VI gave similar permissions. And Pope St John Paul II allowed large number of married former Anglican priests in America and England to be ordained as diocesan priests by an indult that still obtains. But in November 2009 Pope Benedict XVI went further to realise the plans of de Lisle and his seventeenth century antecedents, which Newman said would rejoice him, by issuing the Apostolic Constitution *Anglicanorum coetibus*, explaining: 'In recent times the Holy Spirit has moved groups of Anglicans to petition repeatedly and insistently to be received into full Catholic communion individually as well as corporately. The Apostolic See has responded favourably to such petitions. Indeed, the successor of Peter, mandated by the Lord Jesus to guarantee the unity of the episcopate and to preside over and safeguard the universal communion of all the Churches, could not fail to make available the means necessary to bring this holy desire to realisation'. The Personal Ordinariate of Our Lady of Walsingham was established in 2011 by Pope Benedict as a Particular Church (with its own Ordinary rather than a diocesan bishop) to allow Anglicans to come into full communion with the Catholic Church whilst retaining much of their heritage and traditions, including priests who were married as Anglicans, and liturgies based on Anglican sources consonant with the Catholic Faith. Newman would be surprised to hear Cranmer's dignified prose and prayers in a Catholic Mass, but surely he would not have been troubled. He began praying the Breviary when he was an Anglican, and thought Morning and Evening Prayer from the Book of Common Prayer 'intensely dreary', but he nonetheless looked back in nostalgia on the Communion Service, despite its defects: 'Can I wipe out from my memory, or wish to wipe out, those happy Sunday mornings, light or dark, year after year, when I celebrated your communion-rite in my own church of St Mary's; and in the pleasantness and joy of it?'[19] John Henry Newman was appropriately adopted as patron saint of the Personal Ordinariate of Our Lady of Walsingham. The following year saw the establishment of a personal ordinariate for the United States and Canada, and another for Australia, Japan and Oceania.

While none of these are numerically strong, falling far short of recovering 'half England to the Church' they do show the generosity which Rome is willing to extend to Anglicanism in the search for unity, and the sincere regard in which the Anglican heritage is held. Speaking at the end of his 2010 State Visit to the United Kingdom, during which he beatified Newman, Pope Benedict said the Ordinariate 'should be seen as a prophetic gesture that can contribute positively to the developing relations between Anglicans and Catholics. It helps us to set our sights on the ultimate goal of all ecumenical activity: the restoration of full ecclesial communion in the context of which the mutual exchange of gifts from our respective spiritual patrimonies serves as enrichment to us all'. Members of the Ordinariate reject nothing of the blessings they received as Anglicans and they maintain a spirit of goodwill with Anglicans, and of course communion with fellow Catholics. On pilgrimages to Our Lady of Walsingham, for example, they invariably worship in both the Anglican and Catholic Shrines. Indeed in the Anglican Shrine at Shrine Prayers they graciously pray for the Ordinariate.

Announcing Rome's establishment of the Ordinariate, Archbishop Vincent Nichols of Westminster and Archbishop Rowan Williams of Canterbury, in a Joint Statement on 20 October 2009, said of it:

> The Apostolic Constitution is further recognition of the substantial overlap in faith, doctrine and spirituality between the Catholic Church and the Anglican tradition. Without the dialogues of the past forty years, this recognition would not have been possible, nor would hopes for full visible unity have been nurtured. In this sense, this Apostolic Constitution is one consequence of ecumenical dialogue between the Catholic Church and the Anglican Communion. The on-going official dialogue between the Catholic Church and the Anglican Communion provides the basis for our continuing cooperation. The Anglican Roman Catholic International Commission (ARCIC) and International Anglican Roman Catholic Commission for Unity and Mission (IARCCUM) agreements make clear the path we will follow together.

The Anglican-Roman Catholic International Commission they refer to was formed to further 'our quest for the full, organic unity of our two Communions'[20] after the historic visit of Archbishop Michael Ramsey of Canterbury to Pope Paul VI in 1967. The visit was itself made possible by the Second Vatican Council, opened in 1962 by Pope St John XXIII: one of its principal concerns being the restoration of Christian unity. In Newman's day the Church of England was generally regarded by Catholics (in Newman's words) as 'a human work and a political institution'. One very important development of doctrine that occurred in the Vatican Council, which maybe would have surprised Newman (though surely he would have agreed with it), was in the Decree on Ecumenism (*Unitatis Redintegratio*): the recognition of what it calls 'ecclesial communities' i.e. that Christians outside the Catholic Church are more than a collection of individuals but are 'communities [that] became separated from full communion with the Catholic Church'.[21]

Unitatis Redintegratio developed this further so that instead of simply identifying the Catholic Church with the Roman Catholic Church, it recognises that the Catholic Church 'subsists' in the Roman Catholic Church; while acknowledging that *elements* of the Catholic Church exist in other Churches and ecclesial communities. This does not invalidate the reason why Newman became a Catholic when he abandoned the idea that the Church of England is a branch of the Catholic Church. In *Lumen Gentium* the Council affirmed what Newman believed and caused him to act; that 'they could not be saved who, knowing that the Catholic Church was founded as necessary by God through Christ, would refuse either to enter it, or to remain in it'.[22] A clarification of what *subsistit* means was made under the direction of Pope St John Paul II:

> The interpretation of those who would derive from the formula *subsistit* in the thesis that the one Church of Christ could subsist also in non-Catholic Churches and ecclesial communities is contrary to the authentic meaning of *Lumen Gentium*. The Council instead chose the word *subsistit* precisely to clarify that there exists only one 'subsistence' of the true Church, while outside her visible structure there only exist *elementa Ecclesiae*, which—being elements of that same Church—tend and lead toward the Catholic Church.[23]

Unitatis Redintegratio notably recognised that 'among those Communities in which Catholic traditions and institutions in part continue to exist, the Anglican Communion occupies a special place'.[24] This very much encouraged the establishment and dialogue of ARCIC.

It is hard to imagine how such ecumenical progress would have been possible without the life and legacy of Newman and the Oxford Movement within the Church of England, and his influence in the Catholic Church, not least with his idea of development. His high importance in the Catholic Church was stressed by Pope St Paul VI during the course of the Second Vatican Council, where he was described as an 'unseen presence'. At the beatification of Fr Dominic Barberi, Pope Paul said of Newman,

> guided solely by the love of the truth and fidelity to Christ, traced an itinerary, the most toilsome, but also the greatest, the most meaningful, the most conclusive, that human thought ever travelled during the last century, indeed one might say during the modern era, to arrive at the fullness of wisdom and peace.[25]

The Oxford Movement has enabled the Church of England to recover many of the teachings and practices of the early Church. Looking back over sixty years of the Movement, in his obituary of Newman in the *Guardian*, Dean Church of St Paul's Cathedral wrote,

[He] was the founder, we may almost say, of the Church of England as we see it. What the Church of England would have become without the Tractarian Movement we can faintly guess, and of the Tractarian Movement Newman was the living soul and the inspiring genius.[26]

The Church of England prayerfully recalls its debt to Newman each year on 11 August (the day of his death), when he is commemorated in the Calendar of her Prayer Book, *Common Worship*. The Catholic Church celebrates his Feast on 9 October (because 11 August was already observed as the Feast of St Clare). His Beatification by Pope Benedict in Birmingham on 19 September 2010, and his canonisation in Rome by Pope Francis on 13 October 2019, were warmly welcomed, and the Church of England was officially represented at both ceremonies. Representatives from Oxford University and the University College, Dublin, along with the Minister of Education and thirteen MPs, as well as some peers, were present at his canonisation. The Catholic Co-Chair of the English and Welsh Anglican–Roman Catholic Committee, Bishop Christopher Foster of Portsmouth, commented: 'Both as an Anglican and as a Catholic, his contribution to theology, to education and to the modelling of holiness resonates to this day around the world'.

The Prince of Wales represented the Queen, and gave a fine lecture entitled 'The Harmony of Difference', in Rome on the eve of the canonisation (the Preface of this book). The King, as he now is, celebrated Newman's contribution to both Churches:

> In the age when he lived, Newman stood for the life of the spirit against the forces that would debase human dignity and human destiny ... At a time when faith was being questioned as never before, Newman, one of the greatest theologians of the nineteenth century, applied his intellect to one of the most pressing questions of our era: what should be the relationship of faith to a sceptical, secular age? ... As an Anglican, he guided that Church back to its Catholic roots ... He gave the Catholic Church renewed confidence as it re-established itself in a land from which it had once been uprooted. The Catholic community in Britain today owes an incalculable debt to his tireless work, even as British society has cause for gratitude to that community for its immeasurably valuable contribution to our country's life.[27]

The Development of Doctrine

Aᴼᴛᴇʀ ᴛʜᴇɪʀ ʀᴇᴄᴇᴘᴛɪᴏɴ into the Catholic Church Newman and his friends moved as a group to a former college at Oscott (later renamed 'Maryvale' by Newman) near Birmingham, which had been provided for their use by Wiseman, who by now was a bishop. Within a year they went their separate ways to prepare for the priesthood. It was decided that Newman and his companion, Ambrose St John should go to Rome, and early in September 1846 they set off. On his first trip through Italy in 1833, Newman hadn't noticed the tabernacle light which burns in Catholic churches. But on reaching Milan he saw the flickering sanctuary light inviting him to enter its churches and pray. It made a huge impression on him and became a main topic in his letters for a while. 'Wherever I enter a Catholic church, the Lord is waiting for me', he wrote. 'It is so very great a blessing to be able to go into the churches as we walk in the city—always open with large ungrudging kindness ... all open for the passer-by to make his own by kneeling at them.'

They arrived in Rome and made a pilgrimage to the tomb of St Peter, before going on to the Propaganda Fide College near the Spanish Steps (today the Congregation for the Evangelisation of Peoples). Newman had told Wiseman that he wanted to 'be strictly under obedience and discipline for a time', and the College was regarded as one of the strictest in Rome. What impressed him most was the calibre of his fellow students from all over the world, some certain to be martyred when they returned home.

Newman was essentially a humble man, and though he felt his teachers were lacking in originality and had a deep suspicion of change, he showed not the slightest impatience, being just glad to be there. He simply felt he had a lot to learn. He wrote in his diary that he was 'happy at Oriel, happier at Littlemore, as happy or happier still at Maryvale—and happiest here'.

Newman was soon to discover, however, that his idea of doctrinal development had not been well received in Rome. For his part he was shocked by the theology taught in the seminaries of Rome. 'There is an iron form here', he wrote. It was a non-historical orthodoxy learnt from second-rate manuals. St Augustine was virtually unknown, and even St Thomas Aquinas was not read. The exception to the mediocre teachers was the Jesuit Father Giovanni Perrone, the most respected and influential theologian in Rome, Professor of Dogmatic Theology at the Gregorian University and later its Rector, who became a good friend to Newman, and engaged in long discussions and correspondence with him. Perrone too was critical of Newman's idea of the development of doctrine, but he became convinced by it and in due course advocated it publicly in Rome.[1] It began to make a major impact on Catholic theology.

In his introduction to the *Essay on the Development of Doctrine* Newman criticised the 'Vincentian Canon'. Formulated by the fifth-century monk, St Vincent of Lérins, it states that Christianity is what has been held 'always, everywhere, and by all' (*quod semper, quod ubique, quod ab omnibus*). As a definition of Catholicity, it was widely used by both Catholics and Anglicans, and appears in the documents of the Council of Trent (1545) and the First Vatican Council (1870). But the nineteenth century saw the rise of historical understanding, and Newman pointed out that the Vincentian Canon does not stand up to historical investigation. He went so far as to warn that it is 'native to the Anglican mind, which takes up a middle position, neither discarding the Fathers nor acknowledging the Pope'.[2]

Significantly the Vincentian Canon was not mentioned in the Second Vatican Council, and Joseph Ratzinger, a *peritus* at the Council, later a Cardinal and Prefect of the Congregation for the Doctrine of the Faith, before being elected pope, explained why. He declared that it is no longer 'an authentic representative of the Catholic idea of tradition' for [Vincent's] static *semper* (always) is not 'the right way of expressing this problem'. He stated that our 'new orientation simply expresses our deeper knowledge of the problem of historical understanding'.[3] This was what Newman had explained a century earlier.

The most immediate consequence of Newman's insight into doctrinal development came with the definition of Our Lady's Immaculate Conception. Giovanni Perrone was involved in the preparatory work for the definition, and also in drafting the Bull *Ineffabilis Deus* by which Pope Pius IX defined it on 8 December 1854. Newman's idea of development enabled Perrone to show how, though not *explicitly* mentioned by early authors, the doctrine was implied from the beginning. 'This pious doctrine [was] like a certain hidden embryo, neither brought out by complete voice, nor by many at first; and it appeared while life ebbs away to be unfolded gradually, then better to seize growth, and at last to be seen very nearly in the mouths of all'.[4]

Newman may have been the first to articulate the development of doctrine (in 1845), but Pope Pius IX endorsed it firmly. In his encyclical letter to the archbishops and bishops of Austria, *Singulari Quidem*, he declared in 1856:

> We should not conclude that religion does not progress in the Church of Christ. There is great progress! But it truly is the progress of faith, which does not change. The intelligence, wisdom, and knowledge of everybody should grow and progress, like that of the whole Church of the ages. In this way we might understand what we used to believe obscurely; in this way posterity emphatically might have the joy of understanding what used to be revered without understanding.[5]

That doctrines develop is the underlying assumption behind the Second Vatican Council's *Lumen Gentium*, in which the primary image of the Church is not that of a static institution but of the pilgrim people of God, journeying in the history of the world. It is clearly expressed in *Dei Verbum* that

> The Tradition that comes from the Apostles makes progress in the Church with the help of the Holy Spirit. There is a growth in insight into the realities and words that are being passed on. This comes about in various ways. It comes through the contemplation and study of believers, who ponder these things in their hearts (cf. Luke 2:19, 51) ... Thus as the centuries go by, the Church is always advancing towards the plenitude of divine truth until eventually the words of God are fulfilled in her.[6]

Acknowledging the debt the Church owes to Newman, Cardinal Ratzinger wrote in 1986:

> A body remains identical with itself precisely by continuously becoming new in the process of life. For Cardinal Newman the notion of development was the bridge to his conversion to Catholicism. While I believe that it numbers among the decisive and fundamental concepts of Catholicism, it is far from having been considered adequately, even though the Second Vatican Council has the merit of having formulated it for the first time in a solemn magisterial document. Whoever wishes to cling to the literal test of Scripture or to the forms of the patristic Church banishes Christ into the past. The result is either an entirely sterile faith that has nothing to say to the present, or an arbitrary act that skips over two thousand years of history, throwing them into the waste-bin of failures, and then concocting how Christianity — according to Scripture or according to Jesus — should really look.[7]

Cardinal Ratzinger recognised that the notion of development was fundamental for Newman. Newman famously said in his *Essay*, 'In a higher world it is otherwise, but here below to live is to change, and to be perfect is to have changed often.'

In 2005, during his first Christmas address to the Curia, Pope Benedict extolled the 'hermeneutic of reform', explaining that development in continuity with tradition—rather than rupture—was the guiding principle of Vatican II. He explained that 'where this hermeneutic had been applied it had borne new life and new fruit, and achieved renewal in the continuity of the . . . Church which the Lord has given to us'.[8] Newman's teaching has now been so readily assimilated that it is easy to forget how revolutionary it seemed at the time. Protestants saw themselves as disciples of St Paul; immediate descendants of the New Testament, as though all theological writers after his day (except the Reformers) were irrelevant or corrupt. Catholics, too, sat lightly on history, in reliance on the systematic theology of the Church's magisterium.

Development has now been generally accepted in both Anglican and Catholic teaching. Newman's conclusion that Christianity, as a universal religion, develops different ways of relating to the world has been called a 'handbook of missionary adaptation'.

Newman and the Modern World

As well as the challenges posed by the rise of historical consciousness which Newman readily grasped, the nineteenth century saw exciting advances in technology, science and medicine. But the 'Enlightenment' of the eighteenth century, also known as the Age of Reason (which in fact owed much to Christianity), led to a widespread impression that reason had superseded religion, and that faith and science are incompatible, a misconception that persists even today. Two contemporaries of Newman were Ludwig Feuerbach and Karl Marx who rejected religion outright, while a third, John Stuart Mill (credited with coining the word 'agnostic') proposed an ethics based not on Christian revelation as heretofore, but on whether actions produce happiness or unhappiness. God and the Church were no longer being viewed as the ultimate source of authority. Another contemporary of Newman was Charles Darwin who threw the cat among the pigeons (or mankind among the apes) when he published his theory of evolution in *On the Origin of Species* and *The Descent of Man*.

Darwin was accused of denying the account of creation in the Book of Genesis, and his theory was greeted with fury and ridicule by many Anglicans. Since the Bible is the Word of God, Genesis must be right and Darwin must be wrong. Many Catholics too were disturbed, but

Newman was not. He would have been well aware of what St Augustine wrote in the fourth century about the literal meaning of Genesis:

> Usually, even a non-Christian knows something about the earth, the heavens, and the other elements of this world, about the motion and orbit of the stars and even their size and relative positions, about the predictable eclipses of the sun and moon, the cycles of the years and the seasons, about the kinds of animals, shrubs, stones, and so forth, and this knowledge he holds to as being certain from reason and experience. Now, it is a disgraceful and dangerous thing for an unbeliever to hear a Christian, presumably giving the meaning of Holy Scripture, talking nonsense on these topics; and we should take all means to prevent such an embarrassing situation, in which people show up vast ignorance in a Christian and laugh it to scorn.[9]

The reason, for Newman, why there can be no conflict between science and religion, is that both look for truth, and the truth is one. 'As to Physical Science', he wrote, 'of course there can be no real collision between it and Catholicism. Nature and Grace, Reason and Revelation, come from the same Divine Author, whose works cannot contradict each other.'[10] In a letter to Canon John Walker in 1868 Newman seems to suggest that his *Essay* on development may have predisposed him to accept evolution:

> It does not seem to me to follow that creation is denied because the Creator, millions of years ago, gave laws to matter ... If Darwin in this or that point of his theory comes into collision with revealed truth, that is another matter—but I do not see that the *principle* of development, or what I have called construction, does. As to the Divine *Design*, is it not an instance of incomprehensibly and infinitely marvellous Wisdom and Design to have given certain laws to matter millions of ages ago, which have surely in the long course of those ages, those effects which He from the first proposed. Mr. Darwin's theory *need* not then to be atheistical, be it true or not; it may simply be suggesting a larger idea of Divine prescience and skill. At first sight, I do not see that 'the accidental evolution of organic beings' is inconsistent with divine design. It is accidental to *us*, not to *God*.[11]

Newman was a man raised up for his time, and part of his stature consists in the way he responded to its challenges; but the reaction in Rome to his *Essay* showed that the Church was by no means united in how to deal with questions of the modern age. There were two responses in the Church to the modern age; the 'ultramontanist' and the 'liberal', and they were in fundamental disagreement. The biggest danger for the Church, Newman thought, was to retreat into an intellectual ghetto in the face of new discoveries; and this is where, in Newman's estimation, ultramontanism would lead it.

Ultramontanism literally means 'beyond the mountains' (the Alps), i.e. Italy. The word originated in the Middle Ages and has meant different things to different people. In France, it was a reaction against the Gallican tendency to assert the freedom of the local Church. Among some Catholic converts in England it included a liking for all things Italianate and baroque, with extrovert devotions to Our Lady and the saints. Essentially the ultramontanists looked to the pope to define the truth in disputed matters, which indeed has always been part of the pope's function; but not in every dispute or problem. In an extreme form ultramontanism left little scope for bishops and theologians to discuss and discern the truth. 'Let the pope decide' was the ultramontanists' position. From the convert, Father Faber; 'Rome must really govern, animate and inform things with its own spirit'.

The more liberal Catholics disagreed with such centralisation, and it was a disagreement that in one form or another, would occupy Newman for the rest of his life, coming to a head in the First Vatican Council. Where did he fit into this scenario? In his Anglican days Newman excoriated Protestants for exercising 'private judgement'; now, his openness to modern thought might seem to put him firmly in the liberal camp. Yet, on being made a cardinal he declared, 'For thirty, forty, fifty years I have resisted to the best of my powers the spirit of liberalism in religion . . . Liberalism in religion is the doctrine that there is no positive truth in religion, but that one creed is as good as another, and this is the teaching which is gaining substance and force daily'.[12] Newman was certainly no liberal in that sense; indeed he called liberalism a 'great mischief'. He would more accurately be called a 'moderate'. He consistently stressed that Christianity is a divinely revealed faith, and he was faithfully and consistently loyal to the pope; but he was no ultramontanist. He thought, in fact, that the pope and magisterium in Rome, the theologians and the laity should work harmoniously together in what he called a *conspiratio*, literally 'breathing together'. Later in life, in 1877, in the Preface to the third edition of his *Via Media* he wrote:

> [Jesus Christ] is Prophet, Priest, and King; and after His pattern, and in human measure, Holy Church has a triple office too . . . three offices, which are indivisible, though diverse, viz. teaching, rule, and sacred ministry . . . Each of the three has its separate scope and direction; each has its own interests to promote and further; each has to find room for the claims of the other two; and each will find its own line of action influenced and modified by the others.[13]

Cardinal Avery Dulles, commenting on Newman's prophetic insight, wrote:

> '[Newman] is correct in pointing out the diversity of functions and the need for mutual understanding and, at times, for compromise ... If Newman's realism were put into practice, the Church might be spared some of the bitter controversies that have recently arisen over questions such as the ordination of women and the supervision of liturgical translations. It is remarkable that Newman, eager as he was to defend the authority of apostolic office and the infallibility of the magisterium, would also champion so energetically the rights of theologians and lay persons.'[14]

~ 6 ~

Newman the Oratorian

NEWMAN AND AMBROSE ST JOHN were ordained to the priesthood on 30 May 1847 in the Chapel of the Three Kings in Propaganda Fide. Next day Newman celebrated his first Mass in another chapel at Propaganda, on an altar above a shrine of the martyr St Hyacinth. Newman had been troubled by the prospect of re-ordination. He knew that Rome had doubts about the validity of Anglican ordinations, though he himself did not. He did not have 'that utter distrust of Anglican Orders which I feel in 1870'.[1] But he was assured that even though his ordination would not be *explicitly* conditional, the Church's intention always is 'conditional', and that if Rome, for example, had doubts for any reason about the validity of any Catholic priest's ordination he would simply be ordained again.

Where and how would he serve the Church as a priest? Wiseman had suggested to Newman that the Congregation of the Oratory founded by St Philip Neri in the sixteenth century might suit him, and Newman readily concurred. Newman saw in St Philip Neri 'one of the most cheerful, equable, peaceful spirits that had ever been given to the Church' and he reminded him of his dear friend Keble. Philip was known as the 'second apostle of Rome' for his work in Rome when its spiritual life was at a low ebb, and Mass attendance poor. Newman hoped his Oratorians would, like St Philip, 'manage to be cheerful in order to convert young persons'.

Oratories are communities of secular priests living together with 'no rule but that of love', a form of religious life without vows, and they combine pastoral and evangelistic work in towns and cities with opportunities for study and scholarship. Their structure of men living together, praying together and eating together is not dissimilar to life in an Oxford college. With his wry sense of humour Newman said,

> I will say in a word what is the nearest approximation in fact to an Oratorian Congregation that I know, and that is, one of the Colleges in the Anglican Universities. Take such a College, destroy the Head's house, annihilate wife and children and

restore him to the body of fellows, change the religion from Protestant to Catholic, and give the Head and Fellows missionary and pastoral work, and you have a Congregation of St Philip before your eyes.[2]

A month after their ordination Newman and Ambrose St John, along with five colleagues began a short novitiate in the Oratorian House at Santa Croce in Rome. They also enjoyed a trip to Pompeii, climbed Vesuvius and spent a night with the Benedictines at Monte Cassino. Newman found time to write his first novel, *Loss and Gain,* about life at Oxford in the 1820s; a semi-autographical account of an Anglican student's journey to the Catholic Church. Early in December 1847 they set off for England, stopping at Loreto on the way, where he celebrated Mass in the Holy House. 'We went there to get the Blessed Virgin's blessing on us. I have ever been under her shadow, if I may say it: 'My college was St Mary's and my Church; and when I went to Littlemore, there, by my own previous disposition, our Blessed Lady was waiting for me. Nor did she do nothing for me in that low habitation [the Holy House], of which I always think with pleasure'.

He now had the Pope's authority to found Oratories in England. His intention was not to reproduce an exact copy of the Italian Oratories but to implement St Philip's ideas in a different situation. Newman assumed the Oratory would be in London, and that he would be working to influence the *ordo honestior, cultior, doctior* (the more honourable, cultured and learned), but they went to Maryvale, where it was set up temporarily on 1 February 1848, before moving into a disused gin distillery in Alcester Street, Birmingham in February 1849, and finally to Edgbaston in 1852. Here, among the poor, he found his real vocation. It is impossible to overestimate what the Birmingham Oratory meant to Newman. In it he planted his heart; he loved it, and made of it the framework for the rest of his life.

It got off to a shaky start when Wiseman told him that he had allowed the exuberant convert, Fr Frederick William Faber, who had come into the Church with a group of young men he called 'Brothers of the Will of God' from his former Anglican parish, to join him. Newman's community favoured their acceptance but Newman did not think it would work, and he proved right. Father Dominic Barberi, with his wicked sense of humour, christened them 'Brothers of the Will of Faber'. Faber was a popular priest, a gifted preacher and a writer of devotional hymns including 'Faith of our Fathers', 'There's wideness in God's mercy' and 'All for Jesus', which were translated and became popular all over Europe. Pope Saint John XXIII kept 'All for Jesus' on his bedside table, and it was His Holiness's favourite night-time reading.[3] But Faber had a very different outlook to Newman, and he was an ultramontanist.

That alone set them poles apart. Happily, the Birmingham Oratory was growing and a second house became necessary: London was the preferred location, and it opened in King William Street, just off the Strand in 1855, with Faber its Superior. Three years later a property was found in Brompton, which was then on the outskirts of London. Here, Father Faber exercised a remarkable ministry among both wealthy and poor, and Brompton Oratory thrived.

Newman devoted himself happily to the people of Birmingham; to the poor and their children, many of them Irish, driven to England by the potato famines between 1845 and 1851 in which a million starved to death (principally because of British policy in Ireland). Two and a half million fled to England and America, boosting the Catholic population enormously. In anti-Catholic England they were unwelcome for taking jobs. Newman undertook his share of parish work and community duties in the Oratory, endeavouring to form his brethren in the way of St Philip. Writing many years later to Newman, Bishop Ullathorne recalled how in a cholera epidemic at Bilston he asked Newman whether he could spare two priests from the Oratory to assist two of his diocesan priests who were already working night and day. 'But you and Father St John preferred to take the place of danger, which I had destined for others, and remained at Bilston till the worst was over'.

Newman loved his parishioners in Birmingham. After all, his first parish as an Anglican was St Clement's in a poor part of Oxford. His love for them was reciprocated. One day in Birmingham a poor man gave him his handkerchief. Newman kept it and treasured it, and when he was dying he asked that it should be put around his neck.

The Idea of a University

As well as being a devoted parish priest Newman was, of course, by training and experience, an educationalist. 'From first to last ... education has been my line'. As an Oratorian he assumed he would be involved in education. So when he was approached by Archbishop Cullen of Dublin in 1851 to found a Catholic university in Ireland he was delighted, though he made it clear he would not give up his parish work at the Oratory in England. Most of the Irish bishops had refused to support the new Queen's Colleges of Cork, Galway and Belfast, founded in 1845 as a non-denominational alternative to Trinity College, Dublin (which was controlled by the Anglican Church), and Rome had urged the bishops to establish a Catholic university in Ireland. At a time when Catholic and non-conformist students were prevented from graduating at university or being employed there by the 'Test Acts' (which required them to subscribe to the Thirty-nine Articles of the Church of England),

Newman saw this as a huge opportunity to build a first-rate university for English as well as Irish Catholics. He became less enthusiastic when it became clear that few of the Irish bishops actually supported its foundation: nor did many laity back it. It also became apparent that there were quite fundamental differences between him and the bishops on the nature and purpose of university education.

Nevertheless, it opened in 1854 with faculties of law, letters, medicine, and science, and with plans to establish extensive scientific research institutes including technology and archaeology, an astronomical observatory, and departments of philosophy and theology. Newman appointed a brilliant staff, with himself its first rector for six difficult and tiring years, commuting between Birmingham and Dublin, until he resigned. Unhappily, the Government refused it a charter to grant degrees; it drew very few students from England, and in due course was overtaken in 1871 by the abolition of the Test Acts for Oxford, Cambridge and Durham, which then began to attract Catholic students. In 1882, along with Queen's College, it was taken into the Royal University of Ireland. It did however provide Newman with the opportunity of setting out his ideas on education.

By way of preparation he gave a series of five lectures in Dublin in 1852 on the 'Scope and Nature of University Education': these were followed in 1859 with further 'Lectures and Essays on University Subjects'. They were all published in 1873 as *The Idea of a University*, which remains a classic contribution to thinking about the purpose of education. Professor Jaroslav Pelikan called it 'the most important book ever written on university education'.[4]

It is necessary to know that in Newman's day many students entered university at the age of sixteen as he did and read foundational courses in classics and mathematics. But there was a growing debate about the purpose of university education and the need for more vocational courses. Newman naturally recognised the need for such courses, and indeed he offered them in Dublin, where his Faculty of Medicine was particularly successful. But what he defines as a 'university' in the *Idea* is a college that provides what he calls a 'liberal education' i.e. the education of the whole person 'to think and to reason and to compare and to discriminate and to analyse'. He is not using the word 'liberal' in the pejorative way he does when he speaks about 'liberalism in religion', nor does he mean 'liberal arts' in the sense of literature, classics, philosophy or logic. He was not thinking of faculties or subjects at all; but defined liberal education as an 'intellect … properly trained and formed to have a connected view or grasp of things'. It should form in the mind 'a comprehensive view of truth in all its branches, of the relations of science to science, of their mutual bearings, and their respective

46

values'.[5] It is one which takes a connected view of old and new, past and present, far and near, and which has an insight into the influence of all these on one another. It possesses the knowledge, not only of things, but also of their mutual relationships.

> A great memory ... does not make a philosopher, any more than a dictionary can be called a grammar. There are men who embrace in their minds a vast multitude of ideas, but with little sensibility about their real relations towards each other. These may be antiquarians, annalists, naturalists; they may be learned in the law; they may be versed in statistics; they are most useful in their own place; I should shrink from speaking disrespectfully of them; still, there is nothing in such attainments to guarantee the absence of narrowness of mind. If they are nothing more than well-read men, or men of information, they have not what specially deserves the name of culture of mind, or fulfils the type of Liberal Education.[6]

The problem in universities, he considered, is not the number of disciplines but achieving cooperation among them for what he called 'enlargement of mind' and the avoidance of narrow mindedness. His pattern was the old universities of Europe, which were the jewel in the medieval Church's crown, offering a wide curriculum of science, astronomy, mathematics, humanities, history, arts and in particular classics (which he considered provided 'the most robust and invigorating discipline for the unformed mind'), although he took full account of modern subjects and wanted to include them in the curriculum of his Catholic university. Training the mind does not mean studying particular subjects, like logic or the study of 'how to think'. Rather:

> The enlargement consists, not merely in the passive reception into the mind of a number of ideas hitherto unknown to it, but in the mind's energetic and simultaneous action upon and towards and among those new ideas, which are rushing in upon it ... There is no enlargement, unless there be a comparison of ideas one with another, as they come into the mind, and a systematizing of them ... It is not the mere addition to our knowledge that is the illumination; but the locomotion, the movement onwards, of that mental centre, to which both what we know, and what we are learning, the accumulating mass of our acquirements, gravitates.[7]

At Oxford Newman introduced the tutorial system, which, as we have seen, led to him being stripped of his tutorship. Because education involves the 'whole person' he takes it as axiomatic that students should be under the care of tutors who are concerned with their spiritual and moral development as persons, as well as with their academic work. He explains why he regarded it to be important. Students initially amass information, and then quickly learn to think for themselves, but it is not enough for them to simply regurgitate their teachers' knowledge. Education is not the same as acquiring knowledge. Amassing information does not educate the mind. Real liberal education is achieved not by hearing lectures and reading books but through personal relationships and the influence of others. Although Newman wanted students to study subjects in depth, rather than gaining a smattering of knowledge, he was aware that if a student's 'reading is confined to one subject . . . it has a tendency to contract his mind'. They should therefore be exposed to as many branches of study as possible. It is essential for universities to be residential so that students can mix and talk with others studying different subjects, thereby expanding their knowledge and outlook, sharing their understanding and thoughts with other students and with their tutors. By growing to respect and consult each other the young thus contribute their own understanding, and become part of the teaching process. They may become friends with their tutors, even friends for life. In this Newman must have been thinking of his own experience as a tutor in Oxford. He explained his thoughts in *My Campaign in Ireland*:

> The way to a young man's heart lies through his studies, certainly in the case of the more clever and diligent . . . From the books which lie before them the two friends [student and tutor] are led into conversation, speculation, discussion: there is an intercourse of mind with mind . . . In this idea of a College Tutor, we see that union of intellectual and moral influence, the separation of which is the evil of the age . . . Where there is private teaching, there will be the real influence.[8]

The Idea of a University contains a sustained critique of the popular educationalist and philosopher John Locke for whom Newman had great respect, but who 'distinctly limits utility in education to its bearing on the future profession or trade of the pupil; that is, he scorns the idea of any education of the intellect'. Locke advocated eliminating classics and narrowing the curriculum to 'useful' subjects. Whereas, according to Newman, developing 'a cultivated intellect, because it is a good in itself, brings with it a power and a grace to every work and occupation which it undertakes, and enables us to be more useful, and to a greater number'. Universities in Newman's sense are institutions that promote knowledge for its own sake. University education is for 'training good members of society'. 'It is a great point then to enlarge the range of studies which a university professes, even for the sake of the students; and though they cannot pursue every subject which is open to them, they will be the gainers by living among those and under those who represent the whole circle [of knowledge] ... This I conceive to be the advantage of a seat of universal learning ... An assemblage of learned man, zealous for their own sciences, and rivals of each other ... They learn to respect, to consult, to aid each other'.[9] University education is for the formation of the mind and is inseparable from the development of the student as a human being. In Locke's utilitarian school of philosophy the individual

> becomes himself more and more degraded as a rational being. In proportion as his sphere of action is narrowed his mental powers and habits become contracted; and he resembles a sub-ordinate part of some powerful machinery, useful in its place, but insignificant and worthless out of it.[10]

For this reason Newman was also insistent that universities must not be sheltered environments. He was displeased to discover that some Catholic bishops were quite happy when Catholic students were prevented by the Test Acts from attending university, where they might be exposed to 'harmful influences'. Newman's experience of Oxford convinced him that there was nothing to fear.

> A University is a direct preparation for this world, let it be what it professes. It is not a Convent, it is not a Seminary; it is a place to fit men of the world for the world. We cannot possibly keep them from plunging into the world, with all its ways and principles and maxims, when their time comes; but we can prepare them against what is inevitable; and it is not the way to learn to swim in troubled waters, never to have gone into them.[11]

Although it was a Catholic university he was asked to found, and the Church was central to it; its purpose was not to turn out Christians or Catholics, as some of the bishops were arguing it should. Nor did it exist to inculcate virtue, which in any case it could never succeed in doing:

> knowledge is one thing, virtue is another ... Philosophy, however enlightened, however profound, gives no command over the passions, no influential motives, no vivifying principles ... Quarry the granite rock with razors, or moor the vessel with a thread of silk; then may you hope with such keen and delicate instruments as human knowledge and human reason to contend against those giants, the passion and the pride of man.[12]

Newman had already dealt with the secular idea that education can inculcate morality. In 1841 Prime Minister Sir Robert Peel, who thought that education would lead people to Christian faith and morality, opened a library in Tamworth declaring that 'in becoming wiser a man will become better'. For Newman, who recognised the reality of temptation, conscience, the hard work of sanctification and the grace of God, this was nonsense. 'To know is one thing, to do is another'. Newman was exceedingly witty, and made sport of Peel's boast that the library would be open not just to men, but to 'well-educated and virtuous women'. What about women who were not virtuous? Newman asked. They are shut out, yet surely they would be the 'glorious triumph' of this theory of morality through education. Newman explained that knowledge never 'healed a wounded heart' or 'changed a sinful one'. Only Christianity can do this:

> Christianity raises men from earth, for it comes from heaven; but human morality creeps, struts, or frets upon earth's level, without wings to rise ... Christianity, and nothing short of it, must be made the element and principle of all education. Where it has been laid as the first stone, and acknowledged as the governing spirit, it will take up into itself, assimilate, and give character to literature and science.[13]

In the *Idea* Newman includes a discourse on conscience, a subject frequently mentioned in his books and sermons. Here we are given a critique of the subjective understanding of conscience which recognises no source of authority outside the mere will of an individual. When a person does something wrong, instead of guilt and shame 'the mind is simply angry with itself and nothing more'. They have made a mistake, not committed a sin. His words have a very contemporary ring to them:

> [They] are engrossed in notions of what is due to themselves, to their own dignity and their own consistency. Their conscience has become a mere self-respect ... When they do wrong, they feel, not contrition, of which God is the object, but remorse, and a sense of degradation. They call themselves fools, not sinners; they are angry and impatient, not humble. They shut themselves up in themselves; it is misery to them to think or to speak of their own feelings; it is misery to suppose that others see them, and their shyness and sensitiveness often become morbid ... They are victims of an intense self-contemplation.[14]

A Catholic university must obviously have the active presence of the Church but it should be run by laymen and not controlled by the Church. Even secular universities today, Newman would be pleased to know, generally follow the medieval universities in having chaplaincies. Where many students may suffer mental health and other problems, and may think about serious questions in life, chaplains of the different faiths (in addition to their specifically religious and liturgical duties) exercise a pastoral function for all students irrespective of their faith or otherwise.

More than this, ever since the founding of universities in the Middle Ages, theology has had its place in the curriculum because it is a branch of knowledge, but now the recently founded University of London, Newman was grieved to learn, had excluded religion from its faculties. Some were arguing that only empirical and verifiable science should be taught; then, Newman argued, politics, history, ethics or metaphysics would struggle to find a place. 'If you drop any science out of the circle of knowledge, you cannot keep its place vacant for it; that science is forgotten; the other sciences close up, or, in other words, they exceed their proper bounds, and intrude where they have no right'.

The 'human mind cannot keep from speculating and systematizing; and if theology is not allowed to occupy its own territory ... adjacent sciences ... will take possession of it'. Newman accepts that particular universities may be deficient in some subjects while others have specialities, but he insists that it is wrong to deliberately exclude any area of knowledge on principle: universities should be hospitable to any kind of knowledge.

Newman considers that, in his words, the Church should be 'the element and principle of all education' in a university, but admits not all will agree. Newman nonetheless considers theology to be a unifying principle. 'All branches of knowledge are connected together, because the subject-matter of knowledge is intimately united in itself, as being the acts and the work of the Creator'.[15] By theology he does not mean 'acquaintance with the Scriptures' or the Catholic Faith, but receptivity to a voice that is beyond us, to the light which God gives us, so that we are changed by it.

> Admit a God, and you introduce among the subjects of your knowledge, a fact encompassing, closing in upon, absorbing, every other fact conceivable. How can we investigate any part of any order of Knowledge, and stop short of that which enters into every order? All true principles run over with it, all phenomena converge to it ... If the knowledge of the Creator is in a different order from knowledge of the creature, so, in like manner, metaphysical science is in a different order from physical, physics from history, history from ethics. You will soon break up into fragments the whole circle of secular knowledge, if you begin the mutilation with divine.[16]

Theology engages the mind in the search for truth, and therefore encourages an open mind. It promotes a willingness to have perceptions and ideas challenged, and horizons widened, thus preventing the liberal mind from being drawn into, and made subservient to, a closed and diminishing ideology, which will take the place of theology. This tendency may be detected today.

Interestingly it was a Catholic priest, astronomer and cosmologist, Georges Lemaître, who first proposed that the universe began with what came to be called a 'big bang' and is still expanding. His friend Albert Einstein and most contemporary scientists, including Fred Hoyle, rejected the idea, now generally recognised as proven, and favoured the alternative steady-state theory; because if the universe had a beginning it also suggests it had a Creator, which for ideological reasons they rejected. Fred Hoyle later moved away from atheism, saying 'some supercalculating intellect must have designed the properties of the carbon atom'. The irony is that while Lemaître denied his discovery owed anything to his Catholic theology and was based entirely on science, it was actually his theology that gave him an open mind, just as Newman argued it does, while it was his colleagues' lack of theology, their 'closed ideology' that prevented their minds from even considering it, and so for a long time rejected it.

Newman's *Idea* has received considerable attention in recent times. As the King noted in his lecture at the canonisation, it 'remains a defining text to this day'. In the 1980s the historian, Professor Owen Chadwick wrote 'In the last decades of the twentieth century we could do worse than vote an Act of Parliament that every Minister of Education, or vice-chancellor, shall pass an examination in Newman before he takes office'.[17] The philosopher Professor Alasdair MacIntyre explained in 2009 that Newman's understanding of the purpose of education is very relevant in the modern world. While recognising the dominant place that acquiring specialised knowledge through research holds in the contemporary university (which Newman thought should belong to a different institution), MacIntyre contends that the basic tenet of Newman's understanding remains true. He suggests that perhaps the principal question Newman was posing was not, as he supposed, 'What is a university?', but 'What is an educated mind?', and that the purpose of education is, as Newman put it, the achievement of that 'true enlargement of mind which is the power of viewing many things as one whole, of referring them severally to their place in the universal system, of understanding their respective values, and determining their mutual dependence'.[18]

In a damning criticism of the modern university, MacIntyre went on 'whatever universities are achieving, they are not producing educated minds or, to put matters more justly, they are doing so only incidentally and accidentally. And, if they were to be able to rebut this accusation, it could only be because they had drastically revised their undergraduate curriculum, so that every student was introduced and somewhat more than introduced to, say, the calculus and the mathematics of probability, to historical and literary studies, to some parts of physics, certainly to thermodynamics, to the elements of biochemistry, and to ecological and evolutionary biology. Yet whatever disciplines we name in this catalogue, there always has to be something more, namely the communication of an understanding of the various ways in which the findings of those disciplines bear upon each other and so contribute to a larger understanding than any of them by themselves can provide. We should notice too that the teaching of this kind of curriculum will require a corresponding kind of education for teachers, since we shall need teachers of literature who are well informed about biochemistry and teachers of physics who are able to think historically, all of them being at home with the relevant mathematics'.

Nor is this simply an academic exercise. It has the most grave and serious consequences. MacIntyre contends that

> a surprising number of the major disorders of the latter part of the twentieth century and of the first decade of the twenty-first century have been brought about by some of the most distinguished graduates of some of the most distinguished universities in the world and this as the result of an inadequate general education, at both graduate and especially undergraduate levels, that has made it possible for those graduates to act decisively and deliberately without knowing what they were doing. Examples of such disasters include: the Vietnam War, the policies of the United States towards Iran for more than half a century, and the present world economic crisis.

He cites the example of the 1997 collapse of the American hedge fund, Long Term Capital Management. For a short time the collapse threatened the entire financial system. It had two Nobel Prize-winning economists, who were experts in mathematics and economic theory but lacked historical knowledge. Breda O'Brien also commented, 'This kind of disaster is the inevitable result of hubristic belief in the infallibility of one's own speciality and an unwillingness to learn from other disciplines'.[19]

The *Guardian* correspondent, Sophia Deboick wrote in 2019, 'this now classic work is already being turned to for answers in the present crisis, with universities and science minister David Willetts invoking it in a speech to Universities UK, and Liverpool Hope University recently holding a conference on the continuing relevance of the book. Newman certainly offers some useful ways to think about what we want out of our university system today.'[20]

During the twenty-first century there arose the feeling among some university students that they had a 'right not to be offended'. Addressing the problem, Dame Louise Richardson, former vice-chancellor of Oxford said, 'My own view is that all legal speech should be welcomed at universities'. She argued that students must be prepared to 'hear the other side' of arguments and that 'they should, through reasoned debate, seek to change the other's mind and above all, be open to having their own mind changed too'.[21] This is precisely what Newman believed.

The Oratory School

When it became known that Newman was resigning from the rectorship of his university, he was approached by several convert friends to open a Catholic public school. Newman was delighted to help. As well as being unable to attend university, Catholics had been debarred from entering professions and holding public office since the Reformation, but these penal laws had been gradually repealed after the Catholic Emancipation Act of 1829. Some disabilities notwithstanding, they could now enter the professions, but were educationally ill-equipped to do so. There was consequently a great need to improve the standard of Catholic education. Newman opened The Oratory School in 1859 with seven boys, all sons of converts. It was intended to prepare pupils for his Irish university. As with the university, its foundation had ups and downs with the bishops because it broke away from the existing policy of being under the control of bishops or religious orders, but it was soon welcomed not only by converts but by the Old recusant Catholic families in England too, and within three years the number had risen to seventy. Newman remained closely involved with it for thirty years; and it still faithfully adheres to his idea of how to educate the young, and maintains strong links with the Oratories.

The Laity

In the year he founded the Oratory School, Newman became involved with a crisis that had arisen in the *Rambler*, a liberal-minded literary review, owned and written by Catholic laity for laity. Its editor, Richard Simpson, had published an article by a Catholic layman and inspector of schools, Scott Nasmyth Stokes, criticising the English Catholic bishops for not cooperating with a Royal Commission on schools. Bishop Ullathorne asked Newman to seek Simpson's resignation and become its new editor. He needed Newman to restore the reputation of the bishops after Simpson's attack on them. Newman was reluctant to take on the task but in March agreed to be editor until the end of the year. He disliked the often polemical tone of the journal, especially in attacking the bishops, but he was sympathetic to its general purpose. In his first editorial in May 1859, Newman reproduced the various objections the bishops had made about the Royal Commission, one being that the bishops did not consider the Commission to be fair towards Catholics.

On the commission there were Anglicans and dissenters, yet not a single Catholic had a place on it. The bishops regarded it as essential for the Catholic Church to be represented. But this was refused.

After thus supporting the bishops, Newman then gracefully accepted that the *Rambler* had been wrong to suggest (as Stokes had) that the bishops were reluctant to consult the laity about their views on education. The reverse was true. Their Lordships do 'desire to know the opinion of the laity on subjects in which the laity are especially concerned'. He spoke of the misery of any division between the rulers of the Church and the educated laity. 'It is our fervent prayer that their Lordships may live in the hearts of their people'. But, Newman being Newman, ever the stimulator of thought, could not resist writing, 'If even in the preparation of a dogmatic definition the faithful are consulted, as lately in the instance of the Immaculate Conception, it is at least as natural to anticipate such an act of kind feeling and sympathy in great practical questions [that concern them, like schools]'.

A leading Catholic theologian, Professor John Gillow of Ushaw Seminary accused him of heresy; the laity need never be consulted about doctrinal matters. Newman replied that he used the word 'consult' in the way we speak of consulting a barometer about the weather, not in the sense of asking the laity for their opinion. Gillow accepted his explanation. But his good friend and bishop, Ullathorne visited Newman to discuss his article and advised him to give up the editorship of the *Rambler*, as indeed Newman wanted to do. Newman wryly wondered 'whether the Cardinal etc. were seized with panic, lest they had got out of the frying pan into the fire'. So the *Rambler* was handed back to Simpson.

Ullathorne certainly did not share Newman's idea of the laity, and in the course of their discussion Newman recalled that 'the bishop said something like, "Who are the laity?" I answered that "the Church would look foolish without them".' Newman was now unwittingly becoming involved in explaining his views on the laity, and his understanding of the relationship between the clergy and laity, which indeed had been for him a source of friction both in the founding of the university and the Oratory School. Newman never had any intention of becoming a theologian in the Catholic Church. He thought it would be impertinent for a man who had spent most of his life outside the Catholic Church. His *Essay on Development* began only as a personal exploration as he was finding his way into the Church, but had blown up into a bigger matter. Now he was being goaded into writing about doctrine, and in his next and last *Rambler*, July 1859, he published his famous article: *On Consulting the Faithful in Matters of Doctrine*.

Newman argued that the Apostolic tradition 'was entrusted to the whole Church, and it is manifested sometimes by the mouth of the episcopacy, sometimes by the doctors, sometimes by the people, sometimes by liturgies, rites, ceremonies, and customs, by events, disputes, movements, and all those other phenomena which are comprised under the name of history'. It is important however to note that while Newman wanted an educated laity who could know and defend their faith, he said 'the gift of discerning, discriminating, defining, promulgating, and enforcing any portion of that tradition resides solely in the *Ecclesia docens*'[22] (the teaching Church). 'Certainly I admit that when a lawyer, or physician, or statesman, or merchant, or soldier sets about discussing theological points, he is likely to succeed as ill as an ecclesiastic who meddles with law, or medicine, or the exchange'.[23] Nonetheless, examining the beliefs of the laity, the *consensus fidelium*, is one way of discerning revealed truth; and to hammer home the point, drawing upon his earlier studies of the Arians, he asserted that in the fourth century,

> I am not denying that the great body of the Bishops were in their internal belief orthodox . . . but . . . in that time of immense confusion the divine dogma of our Lord's divinity was proclaimed, enforced, maintained, and (humanly speaking) preserved, far more by the *Ecclesia docta* [the taught Church] than by the *Ecclesia docens* [the Church teaching]. . . the body of the Episcopate was unfaithful to its commission, while the body of the laity was faithful to its baptism . . . The body of Bishops failed in the confession of the faith. They spoke variously, one against another.[24]

His argument was historically true, but it did not go down well with everyone. Bishop Ullathorne was not happy with parts of it, nor was Wiseman, who by now was Cardinal Archbishop of Westminster. Predictably, though without foundation, Professor Gillow accused him of denying the infallibility of the Church. Bishop Brown of Newport translated, somewhat inaccurately, his Article into Latin and sent it to Propaganda Fide, Newman's *alma mater* in Rome, which supervised missionary Churches including England. Ullathorne, who had been in Rome and had seen Brown's letters, was told by the Prefect of Propaganda Fide, Cardinal Barnabò, that the Pope was worried by certain passages too. Ullathorne agreed to take it up with Newman and went to see him in Birmingham, but unfortunately he had also talked to Wiseman in Rome, who burst into tears and told Ullathorne to 'Tell Newman I will do anything I can for him'.

On being told this, Newman wrote to Wiseman to ask what the objections were to his Article. A list was made but was not sent on to Newman. He was assured that Wiseman would sort it out, but Wiseman, who was not well, never got round to it. The sad result was that because he failed to respond, Cardinal Barnabò assumed Newman was being disobedient, and he remained under a cloud of suspicion in Rome for the next eight years, until Ambrose St John and another Oratorian went there and sorted the matter out. Pope Pius IX was informed, and questioned Archbishop Cullen about Newman's orthodoxy. After a very positive report from the Irish archbishop, it became clear to everyone in Rome, and elsewhere, that the accusations against Newman had been nonsense, if not slanderous.

The reality was that Newman had been caught in the crossfire between moderate Catholics and the ultramontanists, one of the latter being Henry Manning, a former Archdeacon of Chichester who became a Catholic in 1851, six years after Newman. As a Catholic priest he became a leading ultramontanist. In 1865 he succeeded Nicholas Wiseman as Archbishop of Westminster and was made a cardinal in 1875. He was devoted, as Newman was, to the poor and counted among his friends William Booth, the founder of the Salvation Army. His most remarkable achievement was to negotiate the settlement of the crippling London Dock Strike of 1889, which made him a popular hero. Pope Leo XIII acknowledged his own indebtedness to Manning, and his encyclical *Rerum Novarum* on the 'Rights and Duties of Capital and Labour' reflects this.[25]

Great as he was, Archbishop Manning was not on Newman's side in the controversy over his article *On Consulting the Faithful*. Writing to Manning, Mgr Talbot, a convert who became a papal chamberlain in Rome, declared, 'It is perfectly true that a cloud has been hanging over Dr Newman'. Then giving the game away, and revealing what most Catholics thought about what we would now call the 'vocation of the laity', Talbot went on to say that 'they are beginning to show the cloven hoof ... They are only putting into practice the doctrine taught by Dr Newman in his article in the *Rambler* ... What is the province of the laity? To hunt, to shoot, to entertain. These matters they understand, but to meddle with ecclesiastical matters they have no right at all, and this affair of Newman is a matter purely ecclesiastical'. Damningly he added, 'Dr Newman is the most dangerous man in England'.[26]

Newman was in no doubt that there was a crying need in the Church for an educated laity. At precisely the same time, the Italian philosopher, Antonio Rosmini was being interrogated in Rome for arguing the same, and his book, *The Five Wounds of the Church*, was banned. (In 2007 Rosmini was beatified.) Theirs were voices crying in the wilderness. Clericalism, and the consequent inferior position of the laity, was a weakness of the Church. Bishop Ullathorne did not agree. 'He has a horror of laymen', Newman confided. Newman had explained his position earlier, in 1851, in his *Lectures on the Present Position of Catholics in England*:

> I want a laity, not arrogant, not rash in speech, not disputatious, but men who know their religion, who enter into it, who know just where they stand, who know what they hold, and what they do not, who know their creed so well, that they can give an account of it, who know so much of history that they can defend it. I want an intelligent, well-instructed laity ... I wish you to enlarge your knowledge, to cultivate your reason, to get an insight into the relation of truth to truth, to learn to view things as they are, to understand how faith and reason stand to each other, what are the bases and principles of Catholicism, and where lie the main inconsistences and absurdities of the Protestant theory.[27]

Newman's teaching on the laity seemed outrageous to those in his day who saw the Church primarily in juridical and institutional terms, with rigid rules under the authority of the pope. For Newman the Church was a mystical and sacramental reality in which all receive the Holy Spirit. All the faithful share in preserving and handing-on the faith.

This was undeniably a time of great suffering for Newman, and it seemed to be his lot. He lamented in his journal:

> I am nobody. I have no friend at Rome. I have laboured in England, to be misrepresented, backbitten and scorned. I have laboured in Ireland, with a door ever shut in my face. I seem to have had many failures, and what I did was not well understood. I do not think I am saying this in any bitterness ... It has made me feel that in the Blessed Sacrament is my great consolation ... O, my God, I seem to have wasted these years that I have been a Catholic. What I wrote as a Protestant has had far greater power, force, meaning, success than my Catholic works—and this troubles me a great deal—I am passé, in decay, I am untrustworthy: I am strange, odd ... I must say that the converts have behaved to me much worse than Old Catholics, when they might have had a little gratitude, so say the least.[28]

The converts who particularly hurt him were ultramontanists like Manning and Faber. Some converts even accused Newman of being a 'Gallican' and 'only half a Catholic'. Newman retained the moderate English spirit and, as he said, he had almost the whole of the old Catholic Church in England behind him; the Catholic families who lived through the harsh penal times from the Reformation. Such was the hatred and fear in England of all things Catholic, that a story spread round Birmingham that Newman was married and had shut his wife in a convent. Another rumour suggested he was so disillusioned with the Catholic Church that he was going back to the Church of England, a rumour he publicly and vigorously denied.

In all the aggravation, misunderstanding and calumny he faced both in the Church of England and in the Catholic Church, Newman remained calmly confident of doing God's will, believing that the truth will out. In words that are quite extraordinarily prophetic, he wrote at this painful time to his friend Henry Wilberforce:

> If you attempt at a wrong time, what in itself is right, you perhaps become a heretic or schismatic. What I may aim at may be real and good, but it may be God's will it should be done a hundred years later ... When I am gone, it will be seen perhaps that persons stopped me from doing a work which I might have done. God overrules all things. Of course it is discouraging to be out of joint with the time, and to be snubbed and stopped as soon as I begin to act.[29]

Newman truly was ahead of his time and remarkably accurate in the timetable of his prediction. He wrote the *Rambler* article in 1859, and it had to wait a hundred and fifteen years for his teaching on the laity to be taken up by the Church. This teaching, so long forgotten, was revived with vigour in the Second Vatican Council. The first draft of the *Lumen Gentium*, drawn up on the old lines, was rejected by the conciliar bishops as beyond amending. The one which replaced it echoes with clarity the ideas of Newman: indeed many bishops actually quoted his article in their discussions. What Newman had called for in the relationship between clergy and laity had at last been heard.

> The pastors, indeed, should recognize and promote the dignity and responsibility of the laity in the Church. They should willingly use their prudent advice and confidently assign duties to them in the service of the Church, leaving them freedom and scope for acting. Indeed, they should give them the courage to undertake works on their own initiative. They should with paternal love consider attentively in Christ initial moves, suggestions and desires proposed by the laity ... Many benefits for the Church are to be expected from this familiar relationship between the laity and the pastors. The sense of their own responsibility is strengthened in the laity, their zeal is encouraged, they are more ready to unite their energies to the work of their pastors. The latter, helped by the experience of the laity, are in a position to judge more clearly and more appropriately in spiritual as well as in temporal matters. Strengthened by all her members, the Church can thus more effectively fulfil her mission for the life of the world.[30]

What *Lumen Gentium* taught is still being developed. The International Theological Commission of the Catholic Church, under the authority of its President, Cardinal Gerhard L. Müller, Prefect of the Congregation for the Doctrine of the Faith, published a long document entitled *Sensus Fidei in the Life of the Church* (2014). In words echoing Newman's it says: 'This convergence (*consensus*) plays a vital role in the Church: the *consensus fidelium* is a sure criterion for determining whether a particular doctrine or practice belongs to the apostolic faith'.[31] This is its conclusion:

> Vatican II was a new Pentecost, equipping the Church for the new evangelisation that popes since the Council have called for. The Council gave a renewed emphasis to the traditional idea that all of the baptised have a *sensus fidei*, and the *sensus fidei* constitutes a most important resource for the new evangelisation. By means of the *sensus fidei*, the faithful are able not only to recognise what is in accordance with the Gospel and to reject what is contrary to it, but also to sense what Pope Francis has called 'new ways for the journey' in faith of the whole pilgrim people. One of the reasons why bishops and priests need to be close to their people on the journey and to walk with them is precisely so as to recognise 'new ways' as they are sensed by the people. The discernment of such new ways, opened up and illumined by the Holy Spirit, will be vital for the new evangelisation.[32]

These 'new ways' were affirmed by Bishop Philip Egan of Plymouth, speaking in 2024 about the Missionaries of St Paul working in his diocese. Among the many gifts they bring, in 'the parishes in which the missionaries work, my experience has been that they've retained the faithful at a time of declining Mass attendance and they've managed to work like a conductor of an orchestra with the parish to release the gifts of the laity and to involve them in the life of the parish'.[33]

Many assessments have been made of how the prophetic insights and teachings of Newman, often the cause of controversy and misunderstanding in his lifetime, were fulfilled in the Second Vatican Council. Fr Stephen Dessain concluded:

> At the Second Vatican Council the tides of clericalism, over-centralization, creeping infallibility, narrow unhistorical theology and exaggerated Mariology were thrown back, while the things Newman stood for were brought forward—freedom, the supremacy of conscience, the Church as a communion, a return to Scripture and the Fathers, the rightful place of the laity, work for unity, and all the efforts to meet the needs of the age, and for the Church to take its place in the modern world.[34]

Cardinal Avery Dulles said Newman

> would have welcomed (the Council's) positions on universal revelation, on the centrality of Christ, on the place of Mary in salvation history, on biblical inerrancy, on the indispensability

of tradition, on the authority of bishops, on the consensus of the faithful, and on freedom of conscience.[35]

Newman's foremost interpreter, Dr Ian Ker, considered that he was 'undoubtedly a great pioneering figure towering in the background, of whom the principal theologians at Vatican II were very well aware. There is certainly no doubt that Vatican II upheld and vindicated those controversial positions which he espoused in his own time and so often at his personal cost'.[36]

Bishop Christopher Butler, OSB, who took part in the Second Vatican Council as a major Religious Superior, considered that at the Council 'a first, immensely important, step has been taken towards the vindication of all the main theological, religious, and cultural positions of the former Fellow of Oriel'. He cautioned that instances in the Council of his actual influence cannot be found that are deep or determinative, but added:

> if this is so, it perhaps strengthens the case for regarding New-man as possessing a sort of prophetic charisma, as one who, because he knew of only two absolutely luminous realities, God and his own soul, was able not only to diagnose the evils of his own day but to see beyond them to the abiding purposes of the God of our salvation.[37]

In this, Bishop Butler was echoing Pope Paul VI, who spoke to a New-man symposium in Rome about Newman's prophetic insight into the modern world:

> [Newman] who was convinced of being faithful throughout his life, with all his heart devoted to the light of truth, today becomes an ever brighter beacon for all who are seeking an informed orientation and sure guidance amid the uncertainties of the modern world—a world which he himself prophetically foresaw.[38]

Cardinal Basil Hume, OSB, similarly spoke of Newman's 'prophetic vision—this insight into his own time and into the future'.[39]

Apologia pro Vita Sua

Newman's attitude and bearing during his years of trial and rejection, both in the Church of England and in the Catholic Church, offer an eloquent lesson on how to deal with difficulties and sufferings within the Church. In one of his sermons he had said: 'As we gain happiness through suffering, so do we arrive at holiness through infirmity, because man's very condition is a fallen one, and in passing out of the country of sin, he necessarily passes through it'.[40] Quite unexpectedly an opportunity arose that lifted his spirits, and not only restored but enhanced his reputation. In December 1863 *Macmillan's Magazine* published a glowing review of J. A. Froude's anti-Catholic *History of England*; a review written anonymously by 'C.K.', containing the line:

> Truth, for its own sake, had never been a virtue with the Roman clergy. Father Newman informs us that it need not, and on the whole ought not to be.

Newman wrote to Macmillan saying he was not asking for reparation from either the writer or the publisher . . . 'Nor do I even write to you with any desire of troubling you to send me an answer. I do but wish to draw the attention of yourselves, as gentlemen, to a grave and gratuitous slander, with which I feel confident you will be sorry to find associated a name so eminent as yours'.

Alexander Macmillan did not reply but C.K. did. Newman was astonished to discover that he was the celebrated novelist and poet, a Protestant clergyman and opponent of the Oxford Movement, the social reformer, Charles Kingsley, Professor of Modern History at Cambridge. Rather than admitting that Newman had never said any such thing, he vaguely related it to a sermon called 'Wisdom and Innocence' he heard Newman preach in St Mary's, telling him 'I am most happy to hear from you that I mistook (as I understand from your letter) your meaning; and I shall be most happy, on your showing me that I have wronged you, to retract my accusation as publicly as I have made it'. He ignored the fact that even had there been any truth in it, Newman was an Anglican and not a Catholic priest when he allegedly preached the offensive words. In reality he had said nothing like them in his sermon. Newman wrote again to Macmillan, assuring him that he was not looking for an apology or explanation, but warned that if he intended merely to 'smooth the matter over by publishing to the world that I have "complained" . . . they had better leave it alone as far as I am concerned, for a half-measure settles nothing'. He concluded by saying, 'that any letter addressed to me by Mr. Kingsley, I account public property'.

Kingsley wrote back, 'The course, which you demand of me, is the only course fit for a gentleman . . . [and makes me] feel, to my very deep pleasure, that my opinion of the meaning of your words was a mistaken one. I shall send at once to *Macmillan's Magazine* the few lines which I enclose'. He adds, 'You say, that you will consider my letters as public. You have every right to do so'. But the 'few lines' he enclosed for Newman's approval were: 'Dr Newman has, by letter, expressed in the strongest terms, his denial of the meaning which I have put upon his words . . . It only remains, therefore, for me to express my hearty regret at having so seriously mistaken him'. That sentence Newman, in his reply, said he must retract. The dispute was not that Kingsley misinterpreted his words, but the fact that Newman had never said anything like the words Kingsley attributed to him. Kingsley, however, insisted on his so-called 'apology', and published it was. He had foolishly escalated the dispute to a new level, and Newman consulted a lawyer friend who advised: 'In answer to your question, whether Mr. Kingsley's proposed reparation is sufficient, I have no hesitation in saying, Most decidedly not'. Newman then expressed his deep dissatisfaction to Macmillan that Kingsley refused to withdraw his allegations 'which I considered a great affront to myself, and a worse insult to the Catholic priesthood'.

Newman had no inclination to take legal action against Kingsley; rather did he decide to do as he had hinted, make public their letters, which he did in a pamphlet under the title *Mr. Kingsley and Dr. Newman: A Correspondence on the Question whether Dr. Newman teaches that Truth is no virtue?*[41] Beginning with extracts from Kingsley's review in *Macmillan's Magazine*, and reproducing their correspondence with his own witty interpretations of it he concluded with a masterpiece of satire, so loved by the Victorians. He called it 'Reflections on the above':

> Mr. Kingsley begins then by exclaiming, — 'O the chicanery, the wholesale fraud, the vile hypocrisy, the conscience-killing tyranny of Rome! We have not far to seek for an evidence of it. There's Father Newman to wit: one living specimen is worth a hundred dead ones. He, a Priest writing of Priests, tells us that lying is never any harm.'

Encouraged by his friends, Newman circulated the pamphlet around the London Clubs including the Athenaeum, and it became a sensation. Ridiculed and rattled, Kingsley was tipped over the top. In a tirade entitled 'What, then, does Dr. Newman mean?' he launched an attack against Catholicism, Catholic priests and Newman in particular. His trenchant pen touched on 'saints and miracles', 'holy nuns and monks' and Newman's 'objectionable and dangerous sermons'. Newman's teaching 'spread misery and shame into many an English home'. 'How art thou fallen from heaven, O Lucifer, son of the Morning!' 'Yes—I am afraid that I must say it once more—Truth is not honoured among these men [Catholic priests] for its own sake. There are, doubtless, pure and noble souls among them, superior, through the grace of God, to the official morality of their class: but in their official writings, and in too much of their official conduct, the great majority seem never, for centuries past, to have perceived that truth is the capital virtue, the virtue of all virtues.'

Newman confided to a friend that 'The whole strength of what he says ... lies in the antecedent prejudice that I was a Papist while I was an Anglican ... The only way in which I can destroy this, is to give my history, and the history of my mind, from 1822 or earlier, down to 1845.'⁴² And this is what he did.

The suspicion had constantly smeared the Oxford Movement, that it was actually a devious and treacherous attempt by Roman Catholics to undermine the Church of England. Newman was a deceiver, a Roman Catholic all the time pretending to be an Anglican. Newman was glad to put the record straight. He did so in a book he wrote in a few months and published in weekly parts between April and June 1864. It became his most famous book, a best-seller still: *Apologia pro Vita Sua*. It is not an autobiography, and you learn few biographical details about the man: it is, as he called it, 'a history of my religious opinions' and the reasons why eventually it became incumbent on him to become a Catholic. In every line of it people recognised his sincerity.

The book brought him adulation: friendships were restored with Anglican friends who had shunned him; the Old Catholics of England, who had suffered so much calumny down the centuries, felt rehabilitated. Newman worked wonders for the Catholic cause in England, dispelled the hostile myths, and restored his own reputation and integrity. There is even a happy postscript to the story of Kingsley. In 1875 Newman was shocked to hear Kingsley had died, aged only 55. He could honestly say he had never felt anger against him. A few years earlier Kingsley had preached a sermon in Chester Cathedral, speaking of Newman 'in a kindly if critical way'. By his 'passionate attack' on him Kingsley had inadvertently become one of my 'best friends whom I always wished to shake hands with when living, and towards whose memory I have much tenderness'.⁴³ He said Mass for his soul.

The shadow left by controversies in Newman's life was being dispelled. But not everyone was happy. Cardinal Manning disliked the *Apologia* because it made Newman and his moderate Catholicism more influential.

Il Risorgimento

In the centre of Rome stands a huge marble monument, scathingly known as the 'Wedding Cake' or 'Typewriter'. It celebrates the long-planned unification or *Risorgimento* of Italy in 1871, and honours united Italy's first king, Victor Emmanuel II. Up to then the regions in Italy comprised separate city-states, like the Papal States, the Venetian Republic, the Republic of Florence, the Duchy of Milan, the Kingdom of Naples and the Kingdom of Sicily. The loss of the Papal States and their merging into a united Italy was a big issue for the Church. Their history formally began in 756 when the Frankish King Pippin III, the father of Charlemagne, gave Pope Stephen II large territories in central Italy. But in reality they went back to the sixth century with the fall of the ancient Western Roman Empire, when the people looked to the popes to protect them from barbarian invasions, and to rescue from chaos the administration of Rome and its surrounding area. Pope Gregory the Great (590–604), a former Prefect of Rome in the civil administration before becoming a monk, was called out of his monastery and elected pope, with one of his tasks to save the population from famine.

He reorganised the Church's lands to maximise their income for this purpose and appointed deacons to distribute food. From then on the popes became the *de facto* rulers of Rome until 1871.

Pope Pius IX refused to accept the loss of the Papal States and the end of his temporal power. The Papal States were dynastic rights, 'the rights of all Catholics' and the pope could not concede what was not his. The issue remained unresolved until the Lateran Treaty of 1929.

Cardinal Manning and the ultramontanists strongly supported Pius IX and believed the temporal power of the pope, as well as his spiritual authority, to be God-given. This was really what ultramontanism was all about. Between 1861 and 1862 Manning gave no fewer than ten lectures on the subject, the first four of which were dedicated to Newman. Ironically he explained the emergence of the pope's temporal powers using the same argument that Newman used in his *Essay on the Development of Doctrine*; that they were implicit in the divine mission of the Church from the beginning.

In his lecture, *The Present Crisis of the Holy See,* Manning painted an alarming picture of the future. Ever since the beginnings of Christian Europe 'the political order of the world rested upon the Incarnation of our Lord Jesus Christ . . . Rome and the Roman States are the inheritance of the Incarnation. The world is resolved to drive the Incarnation off the earth . . . The dethronement of the Vicar of Christ is the dethronement of the hierarchy of the universal Church, and the public rejection of the Presence and Reign of Jesus.'[44] In *The Temporal Power of the Vicar of Jesus Christ* he verged on the apocalyptic: The loss was so grave that 'when the civil powers of the world shall desecrate themselves to lose their relation to Christianity, they will inaugurate the beginning of the last times, when Antichrist shall come'.[45]

Newman was dispassionate about the pope's temporal power. The pope's real power was in his spiritual and pastoral office, and 'that being the case, we are sure that if his temporal power is curtailed, there is some providential purpose in it'.[46] To Manning this was unacceptable. He dreaded the possibility of the pope becoming like the Patriarch of Moscow, or like the Archbishop of Canterbury forced to take an act of allegiance to the sovereign. In the end the Lateran Treaty by which the

Vatican City was established as an independent State, the smallest in the world, gave the pope independence, and the huge benefit of not being beholden or subjugated to the government of Italy or any other country. This freedom has served the Church well, and it could be said that although Newman proved to be right, Manning was not wrong.

The First Vatican Council

It was against this background of changing politics in Italy, and wars and revolutions in 19th century Europe, that Pius IX told his advisers in 1864 he had long been thinking of convening an Ecumenical Council to discuss the challenges of the modern world: 'an extraordinary remedy to the extraordinary needs of the Christian world'.[47] The 'Christendom of Christian Kingdoms is of the past'. The Church had to find a way forward in a different world, and the pope gave time for bishops and theologians to discuss the issues and plan the Council's agenda.

Newman was invited by the Pope to be a theologian-consultant, and he was pressed to accept by Bishop Brown of Newport, whose opinion of him changed after reading *The Dream of Gerontius*, which Newman wrote in 1865. The liberal American Bishop Dupanloup of Orleans wanted him to be his personal theologian at the Council. Newman was very touched, but had no desire to take part either in the preliminary discussions, or to attend the Council. He pleaded age and infirmity. 'I am a broken-kneed pony'. And he said he was not at his best in committees.

The battle lines between the ultramontanists and the moderates really were now drawn. It was clear that Pius IX wanted the Council to strengthen the authority of the papacy as a bulwark against secularism, rationalism and liberalism by defining papal infallibility, a doctrine that had always been believed but never solemnly defined as an article of faith. After becoming a Catholic Newman accepted papal infallibility because it followed from the infallibility of the Catholic Church which he had come to believe in while still an Anglican. Manning, on the other hand, was convinced that the infallibility of the pope was what made the Church infallible.

The question raised by a definition was how to determine where the pope's infallibility began and where it ended. Some ultramontanists like Manning were pressing for a definition that would recognise virtually every papal encyclical, every word of the magisterium as binding. Manning renewed his criticism of Newman by writing in 1866 that he saw 'much danger in an English Catholicism of which Newman is the highest type. It is the old Anglican, patristic, literary, Oxford tone transplanted into the Church'.[48] Newman, for his part regretted that the prospect of the definition was causing in England a resurgence of 'no popery' and might stop the flow of converts. Definitions of doctrine were needed only, Newman argued, when some heresy had arisen against Church teaching. This was not the case now.

Bishop Ullathorne wrote to Newman from Rome deploring the ultramontane lobbying, but expressing confidence in the eventual outcome. Newman agreed, and replied in a confidential letter, 'Rome ought to be a name to lighten the heart at all times, and a Council's proper office is, when some great heresy or other evil impends, to inspire the faithful with hope and confidence ... but now we have the greatest meeting which ever has been, and that at Rome, infusing into us ... little else than fear and dread ...When has definition of doctrine *de fide* been a luxury of devotion, and not a stern painful necessity?' He was anxious that past scandals of the papacy would be brought up in the arguments, and he thought that there had been insufficient preparation and study to justify so sudden and unnecessary a definition. He prayed that 'so great a calamity' would be averted, adding nonetheless that 'If it is God's will that the pope's infallibility should be defined ... then I shall feel I have but to bow my head to His adorable, inscrutable Providence'.[49] His private letter was made public. Newman was deeply shocked by its publication but not sorry. He had not intended to intervene in the controversy, but his views were now known. Despite his misgivings Newman remained calm and cheerful, exchanging reassuring letters with his friends about it.

The Council opened on 8 December 1869. On 18 July 1870 the definition of papal infallibility in *Pastor Aeternus* was passed and was so restricted by *ex cathedra* and limited to teachings on 'faith and morals' that it was a defeat for the ultramontanists. It meant, to their disappointment, that the Syllabus of Errors attached to the papal encyclical, *Quantum Cura*, denouncing liberalism, religious freedom, modernism, moral relativism, secularism, and the political emancipation of Europe from Catholic monarchies could not be enforced. *Pastor Aeternus* stated:

> It is a divinely revealed dogma that when the Roman pontiff speaks *ex cathedra*, that is, when, acting in the office of shepherd and teacher of all Christians, by virtue of his supreme apostolic authority, a doctrine concerning faith or morals to be held by the universal Church, possesses, through the divine assistance promised to him in the person of Blessed Peter, the infallibility with which the divine Redeemer willed his church to be endowed in defining the doctrine concerning faith or morals; and that such definitions of the Roman Pontiff are therefore irreformable of themselves, not because of the consent of the Church.[50]

Even so, some 60 bishops opposed it and left the Council before the vote, but all of them accepted it within a few months. (Some Catholics, mainly

German, eventually joined the 'Old Catholic Church' of the Netherlands, which had originated in the eighteenth century.) The Council was due to resume after a summer break, but the Franco-Prussian War broke out, and the Vatican Council was adjourned on 20 September 1870 after the Italian capture of Rome. Pius IX denounced the 'usurper state', declared himself a 'prisoner of the Vatican', and refused to leave it.

Owing to the interruption of the Council the definition was set in an unfinished context. Manning recognised this and wrote, 'It is easy to deceive ourselves, but may we not reasonably believe that the next time the Church meets in Council, whether by the reassembling of the Council of the Vatican, or in any other way, the first duty will be to take up the work already prepared, and to define the Divine powers of the Episcopate, and its relation to its Head?'[51] Newman thought the same but went further. He wrote to Miss Holmes:

> We must have a little faith ... The dogmas relative to the Holy Trinity and the Incarnation were not struck off all at once—but piecemeal—one Council did one thing, another a second—and so the whole dogma was built up. And the first portion of it looked extreme—and controversies rose upon it—and these controversies led to a second, and third Councils, and they did not *reverse* the first, but *explained* and *completed* what was first done. So it will be now. Future Popes will explain and in one sense limit their own power.[52]

Prophetically, as he envisaged, the Second Vatican Council, in its decree, *Lumen Gentium*, did in fact set the infallibility of the pope not only within the wider context of the bishops but of the whole Church, including the laity:

> The whole body of the faithful who have an anointing that comes from the Holy One (1 Jn. 2:20, 27) cannot err in matters of belief. This characteristic is shown in the supernatural appreciation of the faith (*sensus fidei*) of the whole people, when 'from the bishops to the last of the faithful, they manifest a universal consent in matters of faith and morals'. By this appreciation of the faith, aroused and sustained by the Spirit of Truth, the People of God, guided by the sacred teaching authority (*magisterium*), and obeying it, receives not the mere word of men, but truly the Word of God (cf. 1 Th. 2:13), the faith once delivered to the saints.[53]

In 1874 the Prime Minister, William Gladstone, was defeated over the Irish University Bill, and his government fell. Gladstone blamed the Irish bishops for their influence over Catholic Members of Parliament, and later that year launched what he called an *expostulation*, an attack on the decree of papal infallibility, which he alleged compromised the civil liberties of Roman Catholics and led them into civil disobedience. He suggested it meant that Catholics could no longer be loyal subjects of the Queen. This aroused much public sympathy for it didn't take a lot to stir up hostility against Catholics. Gladstone thought the ultramontanists had achieved their objective at the Council, requiring obedience to every word and decree of the pope. Newman was urged to reply to this, and he did so, with some reluctance, in a long pamphlet in the form of a *Letter to the Duke of Norfolk*, the young leading Catholic layman of the day. He did so with great courtesy, which won him the thanks and congratulations of his old friend, Gladstone. He began by apologising for the ultramontanists 'who for years past have conducted themselves as if no responsibility attached to wild words and overbearing deeds . . . and who at length, having done their best to set the house on fire, leave to others the task of putting out the flame'. He reminded Gladstone that the pope actually interferes in people's lives less than the State does. The *Letter* offers a nuanced explanation of papal infallibility, and an exposition of conscience, which in all things is supreme. The Church is infallible because its revealed message is infallible and true.

> To the apostles the whole revelation was given, by the Church it is transmitted; no simply new truth has been given to us since St John's death; the one office of the Church is to guard 'that noble deposit' of truth, as St Paul speaks to Timothy, which the apostles bequeathed to her, in its fullness and integrity.[54]

The Holy Spirit guides the Church, and the Holy Spirit protects it against error, but its authorities do not always obey it fully, and are not safe from the lesser consequences of human frailty.

> Was Gregory XIII [infallible] when he had a medal struck in honour of the Bartholomew massacre? or Paul IV in his conduct towards Elizabeth? or Sixtus V when he blessed the Armada? or Urban VIII when he persecuted Galileo? No Catholic ever pretends that these Popes were infallible in these acts.[55]

Catholics do not believe that 'Popes are never in the wrong and are never to be resisted'. Newman is unequivocal. 'There are extreme cases in which conscience may come into collision with the word of a Pope, and is to be followed in spite of that word'. And in his famous aphorism:

> If I am obliged to bring religion into after-dinner toasts (which indeed does not seem quite the thing) I shall drink — to the Pope, if you please, — still, to Conscience first, and to the Pope afterwards.[56]

These words have led some to suppose that Newman was a proponent of 'loyal dissent', an advocate of 'private judgement' and a religious liberal, which could not be further from the truth. Conscience, for Newman, does not mean what people often take it to mean, just a personal opinion or choice.

> They do not even pretend to go by any moral rule, but they demand, what they think is an Englishman's prerogative, for each to be his own master in all things, and to profess what he pleases, asking no one's leave, and accounting priest or preacher, speaker or writer, unutterably impertinent, who dares to say a word against his going to perdition, if he like it, in his own way.[57]

As Pope St John Paul II explained, Newman teaches conscience is not a 'sense of propriety, self-respect or good taste, formed by general culture, education and social customs'.[58] Newman himself wrote:

> When conscience does have the right of opposing the supreme, though not infallible authority of the Pope, it must be something more than that miserable counterfeit which . . . now goes by the name. If in a particular case it is to be taken as a sacred and sovereign monitor, its dictate, in order to prevail against the voice of the Pope, must follow upon serious thought, prayer, and all available means of arriving at a right judgment on the matter in question . . . He must vanquish that mean, ungenerous, selfish, vulgar spirit of his nature, which, at the very first rumour of a command, places itself in opposition to the Superior who gives it, asks itself whether he is not exceeding his right, and rejoices, in a moral and practical matter to commence with scepticism. He must have no wilful determination to exercise a right of thinking, saying, doing just what he pleases, the question of truth and falsehood, right and wrong.[59]

An Essay in Aid of a Grammar of Assent

In the same year as the Vatican Council ended, 1870, Newman published what he regarded as his greatest work, *An Essay in Aid of a Grammar of Assent*. The *Grammar* had been twenty years gestating, and is his most difficult work to understand. It is impossible to do it justice in a small compass. His friend, the Jesuit poet Gerard Manley Hopkins, suggested 'it is perhaps heavy reading'; and he offered to write a commentary on it, but Newman replied 'I do not feel the need of it'. A second time he pressed, only to receive the witty riposte, 'to say that a comment may be appended to my small book because one may be made on Aristotle ought to make me blush purple!'[60]

Newman's life work, first as an Anglican and then as a Catholic, turned out to be investigating the question: 'how can the Church relate to the contemporary world?' 'How can people in a sceptical age believe?'

He was sympathetic to the reasons why people found it difficult to believe; he knew many who didn't of course, his brother Charles among them, and friends like William Froude. As a fourteen-year-old he tells us in his *Apologia* that he read Paine's Tracts against the Old Testament, and found pleasure in thinking of the objections which were contained in them. He read some of Hume's *Essays* (unless, he avers, that was a brag to his father!), and 'copied out some French verses, perhaps Voltaire's, against the immortality of the soul, and saying to myself something like 'How dreadful, but how plausible.'[61] As Carol Zaleski observed, Newman 'could readily understand how casting off the faith might feel like a liberation, as if a great weight were removed. To this feeling ... religion needs to offer a "counter-fascination". From Saint Philip Neri, the joyful sixteenth-century father of the Congregation of the Oratory, Newman learned that it was better to reply "not with argument, not with science, not with protests and warnings ... by the recluse or the preacher, but by means of the great counter-fascination of purity and truth", the attractive beauty of the Christian life.'[62]

The *Grammar* was the culmination of his thinking about the relationship between Faith and Reason. There were well-intentioned theologians and thinkers in the nineteenth century who tried by reason and intellectual argument to 'prove' Christianity to be true. Newman considered their attempts to be misjudged. The point to note is that, for Newman, faith involves the whole person, not just the intellect. Faith cannot be discovered without the heart being involved, or without the essential moral dispositions. In one of his *Sermons before the University* Newman says that the intellectual approach

> draws men away from the true view of Christianity, and leads them to think that faith is mainly the result of argument, that Religious Truth is a legitimate matter of disputation, and that they who reject it rather err in judgement than commit sin.
>
> Is not this the error, the common and fatal error, of the world, to think itself a judge of Religious Truth without preparation of heart? ... 'The pure in heart shall see God'; 'to the meek mysteries are revealed'; 'he that is spiritual judgeth all things'. 'The darkness comprehendeth it not' ... But in the schools of the world the Ways towards Truth are considered high roads to all men, however disposed ... if it so happen, in a careless frame of mind, in their hours of recreation, over the wine cup.[63]

Newman insists on the personal nature of faith. He thought that the best way into faith is to start from ordinary human experience, not scientific enquiry.

Thomas Aquinas, the great thirteenth century philosopher and theologian, basing many of his ideas on Aristotle, proposed five proofs for the existence of God, which were unchallenged for centuries. Newman accepted these traditional proofs but he confessed they 'do not warm or enlighten me'. Nor was he impressed by the Argument from Design made popular by William Paley, one of the most influential Christian Rationalists, a Cambridge senior wrangler, in his famous analogy that just as a pocket watch has to be designed by a watchmaker, so do the works of nature have to be designed [by God]. 'I believe in design because I believe in God, not in a God because I see design'[64] said Newman. He spoke explicitly of Paley's argument in the *Grammar*.

> I think Paley's argument clear, clever, and powerful . . . but in this matter some exertion on the part of the persons whom I am to convert is a condition of a true conversion. They who have no religious earnestness are at the mercy, day by day, of some new argument or fact, which may overtake them, in favour of one conclusion or the other. And how after all, is a man better for Christianity, who has never felt the need of it or the desire? On the other hand, if he has longed for a revelation to enlighten him and to cleanse his heart, why may he not use . . . that just and reasonable anticipation of its probability, which such longing has opened the way to his entertaining?[65]

Almost a century after Newman, his observation that those 'who have no religious earnestness are at the mercy, day by day, of some new argument' was illustrated when Paley was criticised by Professor Richard Dawkins, Britain's prominent atheist, in his influential *The Blind Watchmaker* in 1986, arguing that Paley's watch analogy fails because it does not distinguish between the complexity of living organisms that reproduce themselves and can become more complex over time, with inanimate objects like a watch that cannot pass on any reproductive changes. This challenge to Paley (which itself has been challenged by others, of course, as intellectual arguments are) would have occasioned Newman no surprise, which is why he was looking for an alternative way forward in the *Grammar*. It is not real faith if someone is 'converted' by one book and then 'unconverted' by the next. At its best, reason leads only to theism or natural religion, not faith. It limits faith to an intellectual acceptance of 'articles of faith'. Faith is a relationship with God that a person must desire, seek and live. Faith is both reasonable and rational, but it is not the outcome of intellectual study or reason. Besides, being a theist rather than an atheist tells us nothing about the God we love and worship. For these reasons Newman repeatedly declined warm invitations to join the Metaphysical Society, founded in 1869 by notable Christian intellectuals of different persuasions to engage with science. It soon included Prime Minister William Gladstone, Alfred Lord Tennyson, Lord Balfour, Anglican bishops and clergymen, as well as Catholic converts like Manning and William George Ward. Notable philosophers, mathematicians and scientists joined, and prominent non-believers like Thomas Huxley, Frederick Harrison and William Clifford, the Positivists. They met monthly to read learned papers to each other, and discuss them. Newman was uninterested, because for him the difference between belief and unbelief was a chasm that could not be bridged by the intellect alone without 'due attention to one's conscience and moral sense', as he wrote in the *Grammar*.

There are theologians and philosophers today who are less critical of the classical and philosophical arguments for belief than Newman was,[66] but Newman was looking for another starting point. He considered that there must be a different way, otherwise those who are uneducated or unable to grapple with philosophical arguments would never be able to believe, yet they clearly do. He sets out to show how it is possible to believe what you cannot understand. In the *Apologia* he spoke of the existence of God being 'as certain to me as the certainty of my own existence', adding 'though when I try to put the grounds of that certainty into logical shape I find a difficulty': this, Newman now attempts to do in the *Grammar*.

In the first part of the *Grammar* (it is in essence two books), he expanded at length his teaching on conscience, which had been the subject of countless sermons and other work over the years. This great intellectual put his emphasis on the human heart, and on the fact that every human being has a conscience. Conscience is the place to begin if a person wants to have faith. The faith of believers is rational but is not based on reason. 'Faith is not primarily reasonable because we trust a cleric, the scriptures, or even the Church'. A person who doubts the existence of God will not find the answer by reasoning it out, but by listening to and obeying their conscience.

The existence of conscience is a fact. It is a 'constituent element of the mind'. Not only is it a faculty which enables a person to distinguish between right and wrong, it inspires a person to do good and even devote their life to doing good. It exerts a pull on a person to avoid evil. In this sense it is like the voice of someone external and superior to ourselves. Newman calls it 'the connecting principle between the creature and his Creator'. 'Were it not for this voice, speaking so clearly in my conscience and my heart, I should be an atheist, or a pantheist or a polytheist when I looked into the world',[67] Newman avowed. Søren Kierkegaard, the Father of Existentialism, likewise regarded conscience as a proof of the existence of God:

> A man could not have anything upon his conscience if God did
> not exist, for the relationship between the individual and God,
> the God-relationship, is the conscience, and that is why it is so

terrible to have even the least thing upon one's conscience, because one is immediately conscious of the infinite weight of God.[68]

Nowhere does Newman explain more tenderly what he means by conscience than in his novel, *Callista*, where the young martyr is asked by her interrogator what she means by 'God'.

> 'Well,' she said, 'I feel that God within my heart. I feel myself in His presence. He says to me, 'Do this: don't do that.' You may tell me that this dictate is a mere law of my nature, as is to joy or to grieve. I cannot understand this. No, it is the echo of a person speaking to me. Nothing shall persuade me that it does not ultimately proceed from a person external to me. It carries with it its proof of its divine origin. My nature feels towards it as towards a person. When I obey it, I feel a satisfaction; when I disobey, a soreness—just like that which I feel in pleasing or offending some revered friend.[69]

Using words rather like Callista's Newman explains in the *Grammar*:

> [Conscience] is something more than a moral sense ... it is always emotional. No wonder then that it ... always involves the recognition of a living object, towards which it is directed. Inanimate things cannot stir our affections; these are correlative with persons. If, as is the case, we feel responsibility, are ashamed, are frightened, at transgressing the voice of conscience, this implies that there is One to whom we are responsible, before whom we are ashamed, whose claims upon us we fear. If, on doing wrong, we feel the same tearful, broken-hearted sorrow which overwhelms us on hurting a mother; if, on doing right, we enjoy the same sunny serenity of mind, the same soothing, satisfactory delight which follows on our receiving praise from a father, we certainly have within us the image of some person, to whom our love and veneration look, in whose smile we find our happiness, for whom we yearn, towards whom we direct our pleadings, in whose anger we are troubled and waste away.[70]

A person's conscience may be mistaken about some things; it may have been wrongly informed, but we must follow it. Newman is unequivocal. His own spiritual journey owed everything to his determination whatever the cost, to obey his conscience. As an Anglican he obeyed his conscience which at first was wrong, telling him the pope was the anti-Christ, but he allowed himself to be led by it.

> I have always contended that obedience even to an erring conscience was the way to gain light, and that it mattered not when a man began, so that he began on what came to hand, and in faith; and that anything might become a divine method of Truth;

that to the pure all things are pure, and have a self-correcting virtue and a power of germinating.[71]

Concerning those who take no account of conscience, Newman had preached:

> Now, let me ask, if they trust their senses and their reason, why do they not trust their conscience too? Is not conscience their own? Their conscience is as much a part of themselves as their reason is; and it is placed within them by Almighty God in order to balance the influence of sight and reason; and yet they will not attend to it; for a plain reason, — they love sin — they love to be their own masters, and therefore they will not attend to that secret whisper of their hearts, which tells them they are not their own masters, and that sin is hateful and ruinous.[72]

And in the *Grammar*, he wrote:

> I assume, then, that conscience has a legitimate place among our mental acts; as really so, as the action of memory of reasoning, of imagination, or as the sense of the beautiful; that, as there are objects which, when presented to the mind, cause it to feel grief, regret, joy, or desire, so there are things which excite in us approbation or blame, and which we in consequence call right or wrong; and which, experienced in ourselves, kindle in us that specific sense of pleasure or pain, which goes by the name of a good or bad conscience.[73]

What does it mean 'to follow one's conscience'? It is a personal matter, but it has much wider implications that affect others. The role of conscience in showing what is true, right and good and the pressure to act upon it, was evidenced during the Second World War when a group of young students in Germany called the White Rose Group, led by Hans Scholl and his sister Sophie, distributed anti-Nazi leaflets in Munich University.[74] Initially enthusiastic members of the Hitler Youth, joining against their father's wishes at a time when membership was optional, they became disillusioned by their experiences, began to oppose Nazism, and found their way forward by reading Christian writers, ancient and modern, especially Newman.

They spoke out against National Socialism, condemned the persecution of the Jews and were among the few to speak publicly of the Holocaust while it was taking place. They were executed for high treason on Hitler's orders. At their trial, Sophie declared that it was her Christian conscience that had compelled her to oppose the Nazi regime non-violently.

Sophie's boyfriend was a Luftwaffe officer called Fritz Hartnagel, who was deployed to the Eastern Front in May 1942. Sophie's parting gift to him was two volumes of Newman's sermons. After witnessing the carnage in Russia, Fritz wrote to tell Sophie that reading Newman's words in such an awful place was like tasting 'drops of precious wine'. In another letter, Fritz wrote:

> We know by whom we were created, and that we stand in a relationship of moral obligation to our creator. Conscience gives us the capacity to distinguish between good and evil.

Another German student influenced by Newman was Joseph Ratzinger. When he was fourteen his younger cousin, a boy with Down Syndrome, was taken away by the Nazi regime in their eugenics campaign and put to death. After the war, Joseph was very drawn to Newman's explanation of conscience. It became a fundamental foundation for the philosophy *personalism*, 'which was drawing us all in its sway'. When he became pope, he recalled:

> We had experienced the claim of a totalitarian party, which understood itself as the fulfilment of history and which negated the conscience of the individual. One of its leaders had said: 'I have no conscience. My conscience is Adolf Hitler'. The appalling devastation of humanity that followed was before our eyes ... So it was liberating and essential for us to know that the 'we' of the Church does not rest on a cancellation of conscience, but that, exactly the opposite, it can only develop from conscience ... Freedom of conscience—Newman told us—is not identical with the right 'to dispense with conscience, to ignore a Lawgiver and Judge, to be independent of unseen obligations'.[75]

Few of Newman's contemporaries grasped as clearly as he did the threat that liberalism (the doctrine that there is no positive truth in religion) posed to Europe. He foresaw that it would lead first to scepticism and then to atheism, and that Christian rationalists had no answer to it. 'In these latter days ... things are tending—with far greater rapidity—to atheism in one shape or another'.

> What a scene, what a prospect, does the whole of Europe present at this day! and not only Europe, but every government and every civilization through the world, which is under the influence of the European mind ... ten years ago there was a hope that wars would cease for ever![76]

Newman could hardly have foreseen the two World Wars in 20th century Europe, the Holocaust and the grim attempts of both Communism and Nazism to construct atheistic societies, with their attendant persecution and attempted eradication of Christianity. But it is the logic of what he warned about. Belief and non-belief have serious consequences as the

White Rose young people grasped, because the voice of our conscience commands us to do what is right and to avoid what is evil. 'We stand in a relationship of moral obligation to our creator'.

Looking at the lives of the Scholls, and the Church's martyrs and saints down the years, as well as other 'martyrs of conscience' who stand up for what is right, brings home the crucial obligation for human beings to look into and obey their conscience. Conscience brings us into the presence of God as a living person, and that is actually what makes the 'real assent' of faith possible.

This is no dilettante intellectual game of wondering whether to believe or not to believe, fence-sitting, nor an academic discussion about whether God does or doesn't exist, whether to take faith seriously or not. There is an urgency about it. The 'prick of conscience' leads us to take right choices and avoid wrong ones. The very fact that it exists and is experienced reminds us that choices, right or wrong, have consequences, more far-reaching than we may know. Conscience combines a 'moral sense' and a 'sense of duty', giving us an awareness of God's Law and a moral imperative to obey it or suffer remorse. It is such a compelling voice that even people who have convinced themselves that a deed feels 'right for them' in their own situation (as though there were no objective morality), still experience pangs of guilt and shame when they do something very bad, even though they have no explicit belief in God. It may actually trigger a search to find forgiveness in God. And in that search to discover that God is actually searching for them. Newman, in one of his sermons, speaks of conscience as the 'Word within us, knocking at our doors at night . . . who asks for admittance'.

> This is Conscience; and . . . its very existence carries on our minds to a Being exterior to ourselves; for else whence did it come? and to a Being superior to ourselves; else whence its strange, troublesome peremptoriness? I say, without going on to the question what it says, and whether its particular dictates are always as clear and consistent as they might be, its very existence throws us out of ourselves, and beyond ourselves, to go and seek for Him in the height and depth, whose Voice it is. As the sunshine implies that the sun is in the heavens, though we may see it not, as a knocking at our doors at night implies the presence of one outside in the dark who asks for admittance, so this Word within us, not only instructs us up to a certain point, but necessarily raises our minds to the idea of a Teacher, an unseen Teacher.

Being thus aware of the voice of conscience speaking within us, he goes on,

> and in proportion as we listen to that Word, and use it, not only do we learn more from it, not only do its dictates become clearer,

and its lessons broader, and its principles more consistent, but its very tone is louder and more authoritative and constraining. And thus it is, that to those who use what they have, more is given; for, beginning with obedience, they go on to the intimate perception and belief of one God. His voice within them witnesses to Him, and they believe His own witness about Himself. They believe in His existence, not because others say it, not in the word of man merely, but with a personal apprehension of its truth. This, then, is the first step in those good dispositions which lead to faith in the Gospel.[77]

There is, however, another step to take. Newman recognised the need for *certitude* if faith is

to be made the ruling principle of our lives, if our actions, one by one, and our daily conduct, are to be consistently directed towards an Invisible Being we need something higher than a mere balance of arguments to fix and control our minds. Sacrifice of wealth, name, or position, faith and hope, self-conquest, communion with the spiritual world, presuppose a real hold and habitual intuition of the objects of Revelation, which is certitude under another name.[78]

In the second part of the *Grammar* Newman sets out to explore the possibility of certitude: how can you believe what cannot be absolutely proved? In doing so he was defending the faith of the ordinary Christian, and the right of unlearned persons to believe what they have never studied. He was deeply respectful of those who believe without any intellectual arguments. In their defence he speaks of where

Our Lord, in the well-known passage, returns thanks to His Heavenly Father, 'because,' He says, 'Thou hast hid these things'—the mysteries of His kingdom—'from the wise and prudent, and hast revealed them to little ones'. And, in accordance with this announcement, St. Paul says that 'not many wise men according to the flesh, not many mighty, not many noble', became Christians. He, indeed, is one of those few; so were others his contemporaries, and, as time went on, the number of these exceptions increased, so that converts were found, not a few, in the high places of the Empire, and in the schools of philosophy and learning; but still the rule held, that the great mass of Christians were to be found in those classes which were of no account in the world, whether on the score of rank or of education.[79]

He approved John Keble's words: 'Blest are the pure in heart, for they shall see our God'; 'Still to the lowly soul He doth himself impart, and for his dwelling and his throne chooseth the pure in heart'. So how are the lowly receptive to God? How is it that without rational proofs they are able to believe? The intellect cannot be the only source of religious truth.

Certainty in faith cannot be just an intellectual question, not simply a matter of reason. Newman's approach to the question is by a sustained consideration of the relationship between inference and assent. The rationalist approach is to assent only to what can be proved by inference, and that rules religion out. But the connection between inference and assent is not so simple, Newman demonstrates, and in fact is quite rare outside the area of mathematics. We use a whole set of assumptions, convictions and beliefs, which he calls 'the furniture of the mind', to navigate our way through life. We arrive at certitude in ordinary, non-religious areas of life not by logical, rational arguments, but by a kind of intuition made up of previous experiences and events. Everyone does this. It is the normal way of thinking. We do not seek proofs for assents we give and decisions we make. Why do so for religion? If we do so, we predispose ourselves to doubts.

> I would rather have to maintain that we ought to begin with believing everything that is offered to our acceptance, than that it is our duty to doubt of everything. The former, indeed, seems the true way of learning.[80]

If we questioned everything in ordinary life, to take a modern example like crossing a road, we would never move off the pavement. Our minds are constantly reasoning naturally and implicitly, while we are hardly aware of it, from a host of probabilities, previous experiences, hunches and common-sense. Even our most responsible decisions in ordinary life depend on the support not of certainties but of probabilities. Newman, in the *Grammar* takes the reader on a lively journey through mathematics, Shakespeare and politics to show that the normal working of the human mind requires intuition and personal interpretation and experience, for 'the conclusions of one man are not the conclusions of another; those of the same man do not always agree together'. It is the ordinary way we reach certitude in anything.

This is Newman's point: the accumulation and convergence of probabilities, none of which on its own is conclusive, and each of which is personal, produces certitude in ordinary human affairs. In his *Essay on Development* Newman had written about a 'collection of weak evidences' which 'make up a strong evidence' amounting to 'proof'. In the *Grammar*, Newman gave the name, 'illative sense' to this unconscious and intuitive process of the mind by which probabilities (not just in religious matters) combine to produce certitude. A whole host of experiences conspire to 'carry us into' (the meaning of the Latin *illatio*) certitude.

What Newman was explaining is that while single experiences may not amount to much, the effect of an accumulation of probabilities becomes compelling and produces certitude.

> The best illustration of what I hold is that of a cable, which is made up of a number of separate threads, each feeble, yet together as sufficient as an iron rod. An iron rod represents mathematical or strict demonstration; a cable represents moral demonstration, which is an assemblage of probabilities, separately insufficient for certainty, but, when put together, irrefragable. A man who said, 'I cannot trust a cable, I must have an iron bar', would, in certain given cases, be irrational and unreasonable: — so too is a man who says 'I must have a rigid demonstration, not moral demonstration, of religious truth'.[81]

Because the 'assemblage of probabilities' varies from individual to individual Newman avoids giving any examples of what he means, except coincidences:

> Though coincidences rise out of a combination of general laws, there is no law of those coincidences; they have a character of their own, and seem left by Providence in His own hands, as the channel by which, inscrutable to us, He may make known to us His will . . . there is something in these marvellous coincidences beyond the operation of chance . . . I think, then, that the circumstances under which a professed revelation comes to us, may be such as so impress both our reason and our imagination with a sense of its truth . . . especially to those who in addition hold with me the strong antecedent probability that, in His mercy, He will thus supernaturally present Himself to our apprehension.'[82]

Although Newman mentions no other human experiences that lead to an apprehension of God, there are surely others that are very common, especially when we look back on them. An unexpected meeting with someone may prove life-changing; a mistake or failure can turn out to be, as we say, a 'blessing in disguise'; something 'seems to have been *meant*' or 'Someone up there must have been looking after me', are common explanations. Newman does speak of a 'Good Providence' watching over us. Newman was convinced, while gravely ill in Sicily, that he would not die, because God has 'some work for me to do'. Some people have an inexplicable experience like Newman did in the Oratory: he used to sit in a chair on the right side of the transept; one morning he left church before the end of Mass, a thing he was hardly ever known to do. No sooner had he gone, than several bricks fell down from the wall behind him, just on the place where his head would have been, had he stayed.[83]

It happens in human experience that words seem 'written for me'; words of a sermon 'touch the heart'. Answered prayers are another case in point. There are places like shrines where people find a sense of the 'numinous' or holiness; or walking in the countryside or on a pilgrimage feel something 'spiritual'. Many experience the power of prayerful silence at a religious service. An inner voice directs you in some way.

St Augustine is an example. Sitting in a garden, he tells us in his *Confessions*, how he heard what was like the voice of a child in a sing-song way repeating, *Tolle lege*, 'Take up and read; take up and read'. Picking up a Bible from a table and remembering how St Anthony had opened a Bible and acted on the first words he saw, Augustine did the same, and

> read in silence from that chapter on which first mine eyes were cast: 'Not in rioting and drunkenness, not in chambering and wantonness, not in strife and envying; but put ye on the Lord Jesus Christ, and make not provision for the flesh, to fulfil the lusts thereof.' No further would I read, nor was there cause why I should; for instantly, with the end of this sentence, as by a clear and constant light infused into my heart, the darkness of all former doubt was driven away.

Newman also recognises that we often trust information on the authority of others we consider to be reliable, not just in religious matters. For instance, we trust the descriptions of places that we have never personally seen. Trust is essential for co-existence in society. Concerning this, Fr Aiden Nichols, OP, suggests

> there is no reason why we should not regard the theistic assents of others—their grasping of transcendent reality through the particularities of experience—as among the materials on which our own illative sense can get to work. Partly this is because, where persons of outstanding moral and intellectual integrity are involved, we should be willing to let their judgments be indicators in our exercise of illation ... It implies no surrender of our powers of judgment, because in locating such people we have ourselves applied judgment to our impressions of their lives and writings. But more importantly, we can find our own existence and experience illuminated through their intersection with the texts that represent the illative judgments of others in their own particular approaches to God.'[84]

Saints are recognised as witnesses of faith, and Pope St John Paul II and his successors have speeded up the process of canonisation in order to hold up for veneration more contemporary saints who speak to people today: like Fr Maximillian Kolbe who voluntarily sacrificed his life in Auschwitz to save a married family man, and Edith Stein (Teresa Benedicta of the Cross) who chose to reveal her Jewish identity, and died at Birkenau; Mother Teresa, the apostle of Charity in India; Josephine Bakhita the horribly tortured victim of human trafficking who became a religious sister; and most recently the teenager, Carlo Acutis, an English boy born in London in 1991 of Italian parents, who like most of his peers created webpages and played video games on his phone, but lived an extraordinarily heroic life of goodness, before dying of leukemia when he was fifteen. In them we recognize something of what is right and true in human life.

Attending to conscience and to the accumulation and convergence of probabilities will take a person from atheism to theism, to what Newman called 'notional assent' in the intellect, or 'natural religion'. But for 'notional assent' to become 'real assent' or belief from which action proceeds (and Faith is nothing without action) imagination is required to reach the heart. In one of his first sermons Newman reminded his hearers that 'there is no such thing as abstract religion'. He insists on the personal nature of faith, a faith involving the 'whole person', including not just the intellect but the heart.

An intellectual or notional assent, an acceptance that God exists and a creed is true, is not enough. Newman recognised the necessity of creeds and dogmas, otherwise Christianity is reduced to a merely moralistic or sentimental religion; but he acknowledged the part the heart must play in belief. He chose *Cor ad cor loquitur* ('heart speaks to heart'), words of St Francis de Sales, as the motto for his coat of arms when he was made a cardinal. In the *Development of Doctrine* he had written: 'When we pray, we pray, not to an assemblage of notions, or to a creed, but to One Individual Being; and when we speak of Him we speak of a Person, not of a Law or a Manifestation'.[85] He would have readily agreed with the Catholic Catechism that 'faith is first of all a personal adherence of man to God. At the same time, and inseparably, it is a free assent to the whole truth that God has revealed.'[86]

> The heart is commonly reached, not through the reason, but through the imagination, by means of direct impressions, by the testimony of facts and events, by history, by description. Persons influence us, voices melt us, looks subdue us, deeds inflame us. Many a man will live and die upon a dogma: no man will be a martyr for a conclusion. A conclusion is but an opinion.[87]

In a sermon one Good Friday he preached:

> Unless we have a true love of Christ, we are not His true disciples; and we cannot love Him unless we have heartfelt gratitude to Him; and we cannot duly feel gratitude, unless we feel keenly what He suffered for us. I say it seems to us impossible, under

the circumstances of the case, that anyone can have attained to the love of Christ, who feels no distress, no misery, at the thought of His bitter pains, and no self-reproach at having through his own sins had a share in causing them.

I know quite well, and wish you, my brethren, never to forget, that feeling is not enough; that it is not enough merely to feel and nothing more; that to feel grief for Christ's sufferings, and yet not to go on to obey him, is not true love, but a mockery. True love both feels right, and acts right; but at the same time as warm feelings without religious conduct are a kind of hypocrisy, so, on the other hand, right conduct, when unattended with deep feelings, is at best a very imperfect sort of religion.[88]

In Newman's day, and often today, the doctrine of the Holy Trinity has sometimes been considered a mystery (though, Newman pointed out, it is never so described in the formularies of the Church), an unnecessary complication in the rationalists' attempts to promote theism. In the *Grammar* Newman shows how the imagination can take hold of the doctrine of the Holy Trinity expressed in the Creeds so that it becomes beautiful and real. The idea of God being Father, Son and Holy Spirit offers far more profound material for meditation, thinking and praying, than does the word 'God'. The prayers and devotions of the Church are grounded in the Holy Trinity; it holds the believer's imagination, prayer and spiritual life, and in the contemplation of it are found the 'motives for devotion and faithful obedience'.

There is a developing process, Newman tells us, in those seeking faith, taking them from 'the rejection of atheism, then from theism to Christianity, and from Christianity to Evangelical Religion, and from this to Catholicity'.[89] So far as his choice of Christianity is concerned when progressing from theism, Newman refutes the contention that since he was 'educated in Christianity, I merely judge of it by its own principles; but this is not the fact'. He has surveyed the various religions of the world including 'the heathen moralists'. 'Aristotle has been my master', Newman says. 'No religion is from God that contradicts our sense of right and wrong'.[90] Christianity involves morality as well as doctrine, because it recognises that a moral life is essential for being truly human, however far short everyone falls through sin. He affirms that Christianity alone has a definite message addressed to all mankind. 'As far as I know the religion of Mahomet [Islam] has brought into the world no new doctrine whatever, except, indeed, that of its own divine origin.' 'Nor am I sure of any definite message from God to man [in the religions of the Far East] which they convey and protect, though they may have sacred books.' In the *Grammar* there are many pages discussing different religions, especially the Jewish faith from which Christianity sprang in the days of the Roman Empire, including a long dissertation on Gibbon's *Decline and Fall of the Roman Empire*. All this before what he sees to be the logic of moving from theism to Christianity, to the 'central doctrine of Revelation, the Mediation of Christ'. In one of his sermons in the Oratory Newman says,

> You ask, what it is you need, besides eyes, in order to see the truths of revelation: I will tell you at once; you need light. Not the keenest eyes can see in the dark. Now, though your mind be the eye, the grace of God is the light ... Now, you are born under a privation of this blessed spiritual light; and, while it remains, you will not, cannot, really see God. I do not say you will have no thought at all about God, nor be able to talk about Him. True, but you will not be able to do more than reason about Him. Your thoughts and your words will not get beyond a mere reasoning.[91]

People who are drawn to Christianity and seek faith allow themselves to be drawn to the worship of the Church, to the Scriptures, to reflection and prayer. It is not enough to do nothing. It is necessary to use the imagination. There come into the mind images in the Gospel that meet human needs.

Christianity presents itself to us 'both through the intellect and the imagination', not necessarily in that order. Newman concludes his *Essay in Aid of a Grammar of Assent*:

> Christianity is addressed, both as regards its evidences and its contents, to minds which are in the normal condition of human nature, as believing in God and in a future judgment. Such minds it addresses both through the intellect and through the imagination; creating a certitude of its truth by arguments too various for direct enumeration, too personal and deep for words, too powerful and concurrent for refutation. Nor need reason come first and faith second (though this is the logical order), but one and the same teaching is in different aspects both object and proof, and elicits one complex act both of inference and of assent. It speaks to us one by one, and it is received by us one by one, as the counterpart, so to say, of ourselves, and is real as we are real.
>
> In the sacred words of its Divine Author and Object concerning Himself, 'I am the Good Shepherd, and I know Mine, and Mine know Me. My sheep hear My voice, and I know them, and they follow Me. And I give them everlasting life, and they shall never perish; and no man shall pluck them out of My hand'.[92]

(It can be no coincidence that the earliest Christian paintings, and there are very many of them in the catacombs of Rome, as well as the oldest statue, depict Jesus as the Good Shepherd with a sheep on his shoulder; Jesus the Good Shepherd, who declared he had come 'to seek and save what is lost', carrying the sheep home.) This is the image that made the greatest appeal in the early Church, and probably still does.

Newman's approach is much appreciated today. He anticipated the way the New Evangelisation works at a popular church level with its emphasis on human experience and personal testimonies. But unlike some other forms of Christianity, which similarly emphasise human experience and testimony Newman firmly holds to the necessity of the Church and the binding character of dogma, of what God has revealed. The Scriptures are crucial.

A few days after Newman's canonisation, Bishop Robert Barron, the founder of Word on Fire Institute, gave a lecture in St Mary's Oxford, packed as it was in Newman's day with students and others. He was invited to use the pulpit where Newman had preached for twenty years, but declined saying, *Domine, non sum dignus*. His subject was 'Newman and the New Evangelisation'. 'What Newman saw commencing in the nineteenth century has come now rather sadly to fruition, and so as Vatican II implied and the last four popes have explicitly urged, a new evangelisation of formerly Christian lands is urgently needed'. He affirmed that 'other avenues both classical and contemporary may be useful of course', but went on, 'I do believe Newman's apologetic path, intelligent, spiritually honest, psychologically astute, biblically grounded will prove efficacious in our work today; and therefore a rediscovery of what Newman recommended 150 years ago will prove very helpful in the concrete work of preaching, teaching and evangelising'.[93]

He spoke at great length of the value and importance of the *Grammar of Assent* for the new evangelisation, and predicted Newman would be made a Doctor of the Church. 'If that happens, that Newman is named a Doctor, we should really take advantage of that, and study his writings deeply. I think it might help to heal some of the divisions in our Church', he added later.

Faith

In one of his sermons Newman poses the question, 'What is meant by faith'? And he answers,

> it is to feel in good earnest that we are creatures of God; it is a practical perception of the unseen world; it is to understand that this world is not enough for our happiness, to look beyond it on towards God, to realise His presence, to wait upon Him, to endeavour to learn and to do His will, and to seek our good from Him. It is not a mere temporary strong act or impetuous

feeling of the mind, an impression or a view coming upon it, but it is a habit, a state of mind, lasting and consistent. To have faith in God is to surrender one's-self to God, humbly to put one's interests, or to wish to be allowed to put them into His hands who is the Sovereign Giver of all good.[94]

In another sermon he used an argument reminiscent of Pascal's wager:

Only reflect, what is faith itself but an acceptance of things unseen, from the love of them, *beyond* the determinations of calculation and experience? Faith outstrips argument. If there is only a fair chance that the Bible is true, that heaven is the reward of obedience, and hell of wilful sin, it is worthwhile, it is safe, to sacrifice this world to the next ... it were worthwhile on that chance to do it. This then, is what is meant by faith going against reason, that it cares not for the measure of probabilities; it does not ask whether a thing is more or less likely; but if there is a fair and clear likelihood what God's will is, it acts upon it. If Scripture were not true, we should in the next world be left where we were; we should, in the event, be no worse off than before; but if it be true, then we shall be infinitely worse off for not believing it than if we had believed it. We all know the retort which the aged saint made in the story, when a licentious youth reminded him, how he would have wasted life if there were no future state of recompense: 'True, my son,' he answered, 'but how *much* worse a waste is yours if there is.'[95]

That is not to say that Faith is a 'leap into the dark', as some have suggested. Faith cannot be proved or discovered by reason but it is perfectly rational. It is not 'blind faith' to believe, even while being conscious or troubled by intellectual difficulties, or by a spiritual temptation to doubt like the man in the Gospel who prayed 'Lord, I believe, help my unbelief'.

Many persons are very sensitive of the difficulties of Religion; I am as sensitive of them as any one; but I have never been able to see a connection between apprehending those difficulties, however keenly, and multiplying them to any extent, and on the other hand doubting the doctrines to which they are attached. Ten thousand difficulties do not make one doubt, as I understand the subject; difficulty and doubt are incommensurate. There of course may be difficulties in the evidence; but I am speaking of difficulties intrinsic to the doctrines themselves, or to their relations with each other. A man may be annoyed that he cannot work out a mathematical problem, of which the answer is or is not given to him, without doubting that it admits of an answer, or that a certain particular answer is the true one. Of all points of faith, the being of a God is, to my own apprehension, encompassed with most difficulty, and yet borne in upon our minds with most power.[96]

The person with a difficulty asks, 'How can that be so?' whereas a person who doubts says, 'That can't be so!' It is disobedience that turns difficulties into doubts, which would eventually destroy faith.

Faith is something other than intellectual conviction and does not rest on it, as Newman explains in a Sermon about St Peter on the text 'Sanctify the Lord God in your hearts; and be ready always to give an answer to every man that asketh you a reason of the hope that is in you, with meekness and fear' (1 Peter 3:15). This text has been used in apologetics as an approval to seek rational arguments for faith, but it is expounded quite differently by Newman:

> St Peter's faith was one of his characteristic graces. It was ardent, keen, watchful, and prompt. It dispensed with argument, calculation, deliberation, and delay, whenever it heard the voice of its Lord and Saviour: and it heard that voice even when its accents were low, or when it was unaided by the testimony of the other senses ... If in anyone Faith appears in contrast with what we commonly understand by Reason, and with Evidence, it so appears in the instance of Peter. When he reasoned, it was at times when Faith was lacking. 'When he saw the wind boisterous, he was afraid'; and Christ in consequence called him, 'Thou of little faith'.

He goes on:

> Faith and Reason, then, stand in strong contrast in the history of Peter: yet it is Peter, and he not the fisherman of Galilee, but the inspired Apostle, who in the text gives us a precept which implies, in order to its due fulfilment, a careful exercise of our Reason, an exercise both upon Faith, considered as an act or habit of mind, and upon the Object of it. We are not only to 'sanctify the Lord God in our hearts,' not only to prepare a shrine within us in which our Saviour Christ may dwell, and where we may worship Him; but we are so to understand what we do, so to master our thoughts and feelings, so to recognise what we believe, and how we believe, so to trace out our ideas and impressions, and to contemplate the issue of them, that we may be 'ready always to give an answer to every man that asketh us an account of the hope that is in us.' In these words, I conceive, we have a clear warrant, or rather an injunction, to cast our religion into the form of Creed and Evidences.
>
> It would seem, then, that though Faith is the characteristic of the Gospel, and Faith is the simple lifting of the mind to the

Unseen God, without conscious reasoning or formal argument, still the mind may be allowably, nay, religiously engaged, in reflecting upon its own Faith; investigating the grounds and the Object of it, bringing it out into words, whether to defend, or recommend, or teach it to others.[97]

Newman left a huge corpus of writings and sermons on Our Lady together with devotions and prayers, both from his Anglican days and his Catholic. Mary, he teaches, is the pattern of faith, because she said 'yes'. Faith involves hearing the Word of God, pondering it, believing it, obeying it and living it, as Mary did. In a sermon on the text 'Mary kept all these things, and pondered them in her heart' he declared that Mary

is our pattern of Faith, both in the reception and in the study of Divine Truth. She does not think it enough to accept, she dwells upon it; not enough to possess, she uses it; not enough to assent, she develops it; not enough to submit the Reason, she reasons upon it; not indeed reasoning first, and believing afterwards, with Zacharias, yet first believing without reasoning, next from love and reverence, reasoning after believing. And thus she symbolizes to us, not only the faith of the unlearned, but of the doctors of the Church also, who have to investigate, and weigh, and define, as well as to profess the Gospel; to draw the line between truth and heresy; to anticipate or remedy the various aberrations of wrong reason; to combat pride and recklessness with their own arms; and thus to triumph over the sophist and the innovator.[98]

Newman was converted to evangelicalism in his youth and gradually moved towards Catholicism in Oxford. A mark of his transition from evangelicalism came in 1838 when he published thirteen *Lectures on the Doctrine of Justification*, which he had given in St Mary's. Justification describes the way in which God brings us sinful beings into a relationship with him. Just how that happens was a most divisive subject between the Protestant reformer, Martin Luther and the Catholic Church at the Reformation. Newman (writing as an Anglican) tried to steer a *via media* between what he called Luther's 'erroneous' teaching on justification by *faith alone* and what he called the 'defective' (Catholic) theory of justification by *obedience*. He was seeking a convergence of these 'apparently discordant views', which are both partially true. Some have accused him of not fully understanding Luther, and it is certainly true that he uses the words 'Luther' and 'Lutheranism' rather loosely to mean the popular Protestantism of his day, which was often inaccurately claimed to be based on Luther's teaching. This does not detract from Newman's achievement, and he certainly did profoundly disagree with some of Luther's teaching on justification. In recent times his *Lectures on Justification* have been endorsed, among others, by Ian Ker, who considered it arguably Newman's 'most profound and subtle theological work'. He regarded it as 'a pioneering classic of ecumenical theology' and 'an outstanding early example of Newman's many anticipations of much later developments in Roman Catholic theology'. Newman stood by his *Lectures on Justification* after he became a Catholic, and he republished them in 1874.

Catholics and Protestants alike agree that fallen human beings cannot merit God's mercy, nor can his mercy be 'earned' by doing good works, because it is God's gift. Newman's contemporary Evangelicals interpreted this to mean that God justifies us (brings us into a relationship with Him; makes us 'at-one' with Him) by 'imputing' righteousness to us, i.e. counting us as though we are righteous. In other words righteousness is merely imputed, not imparted to us. Catholics, on the other hand, insist that in justifying us, God's grace effects a real change within us. As Newman put it, 'God's Word . . . effects what it announces'.

> Christ's Cross does not justify by being looked at, but by being applied; not by as merely beheld by faith, but by being actually set up within us, and that not by our act, but by God's invisible grace. Men sit, and gaze, and speak of the great Atonement [at-one-ment] and think this is appropriating it; not more truly than kneeling to the material cross itself is appropriating it. Men say that faith is an apprehending and applying; faith cannot really apply the Atonement; man cannot make the Saviour of the world his own; the Cross must be brought home to us, not in word, but in power, and this is the work of the Spirit. This is justification; but when imparted to the soul, it draws blood, it heals, it purifies, it glorifies . . .'the world is crucified unto me, and I unto the world . . . An inward crucifixion was the attendant process of justification'.[99]

Newman wrote: 'How different from the popular Protestant doctrine, which says. "If you have sinned, go to meet Christ in faith, look upon him who has borne the sins of the world, cast your burden upon Him, apprehend Him, apply His merits to your soul, believe you are justified, and you are justified without anything else on your part".'[100]

To explain the Catholic teaching on justification Newman takes us back before the Reformation divide, to the doctrine of Christ's Incarnation as expounded by the Fathers of both East and West, especially St Augustine who has 'the whole of scripture behind him'; and he explains that God's 'indwelling', i.e. His Presence in a person, is a gift of God through Faith, and a reality in believers. It is the transforming effect of divine grace and has been called 'divinisation' or *apotheosis*, literally 'making divine' from the words of St Peter that 'you may become partakers of the divine nature' (2 Peter 1:4). God's indwelling is a constant theme in Newman's sermons. He says, 'Turning to the Gospel we shall find that such a gift is actually promised to us by our Lord; a gift which must of necessity be at once our justification and our sanctification, for it is nothing short of the indwelling in us of God the Father and the Word Incarnate through the Holy Ghost. If this is so, we have found what we sought: *This* is to be justified, to receive the Divine Presence within us, and be made a Temple of the Holy Ghost'.

> Through the participation of Christ we receive, as through a channel, the true presence of God within and without us, imbuing us with sanctity and immortality. *This*, I repeat, is our justification, our ascent through Christ to God, or God's descent through Christ to us . . . And this is our true Righteousness, — not the mere name of righteousness, not only forgiveness or favour as an act of the Divine Mind, not only sanctification within (great indeed as these blessings would be, yet it is somewhat more) . . . it is the indwelling of our glorified Lord. This is the one great gift of God purchased by the Atonement, which is light instead of darkness.[101]

As he preached in a sermon already quoted (page 8), 'A true Christian, then, may almost be defined as one who has a ruling sense of God's Presence with him. As none but the justified persons have that privilege, so none but the justified have that practical perception of it.'

Luther, by insisting that we are justified by faith *alone*, inevitably had difficulty with St James who taught that 'faith apart from works is useless . . . You see that a person is justified by works and not by faith alone' (James 2:20). Luther famously dismissed the Letter of James as an 'epistle of straw'. The practical effect of Luther's teaching is to see little need to make personal efforts: celibacy and poverty (hence Luther's rejection of religious communities), even worship, the sacraments, confession, pilgrimages or retreats are merely human works that avail nothing for salvation.

Newman enlarges on this in a Sermon on the Parable of the Two Sons who were asked by their father to work in his vineyard. 'One answered and said, "I will not"; but afterward he repented, and went. And the second answered and said, "I will go, Sir"; and went not' (Matthew 21:28–32):

> We know Scripture tells us that God accepts those who have faith in Him. Now the question is, 'What is faith, and how can a man tell that he has faith'? Some persons answer at once and without hesitation, that 'to have faith is to feel oneself to be nothing, and God everything; it is to be convinced of sin, to be conscious one cannot save oneself, and to wish to be saved by

Christ our Lord; and that it is, moreover, to have the love of
Him warm in one's heart, and to rejoice in Him, to desire His
glory, and to resolve to live to Him and not to the world.' But I
will answer, with all due seriousness, as speaking on a serious
subject, that this is not faith.

Not that it is not necessary (it is very necessary) to be convinced
that we are laden with infirmity and sin, and without health in
us, and to look for salvation solely to Christ's blessed sacrifice on
the cross; and we may well be thankful if we are thus minded;
but that a man may feel all this that I have described, vividly,
and still not yet possess one particle of true religious faith. Why?
Because there is an immeasurable distance between feeling right
and doing right. A man may have all these good thoughts and
emotions, yet (if he has not yet hazarded them to the experiment
of practice) he cannot promise himself that he has any sound and
permanent principle at all. If he has not yet acted upon them,
we have no voucher, barely on account of them, to believe that
they are anything but words.

Nay, till he acts upon them, he has not even evidence to
himself that he has true living faith. Dead faith (as St. James
says) profits no man. Of course; the Devils have it. What, on
the other hand is living faith? Do fervent thoughts make faith
living? St. James tells us otherwise. He tells us works, deeds of
obedience, are the life of faith. 'As the body without the spirit
is dead, so faith without works is dead also'. (James 2: 26.) So
that those who think they really believe, because they have in
word and thought surrendered themselves to God, are much
too hasty in their judgment. They have done something, indeed,
but not at all the most difficult part of their duty, which is to
surrender themselves to God in deed and act. They have as yet
done nothing to show they will not, after saying 'I go', the next
moment 'go not'; nothing to show they will not act the part of
the self-deceiving disciple, who said, 'Though I die with Thee,
I will not deny Thee', yet straightway went and denied Christ
thrice. As far as we know anything of the matter, justifying faith
has no existence independent of its particular definite acts. It
may be described to be the temper under which men obey; the
humble and earnest desire to please Christ which causes and
attends on actual services.

In a lovely passage he goes on:

He who does one little deed of obedience, whether he denies
himself some comfort to relieve the sick and needy, or curbs
his temper, or forgives an enemy, or asks forgiveness for an
offence committed by him, or resists the clamour or ridicule
of the world—such an one (as far as we are given to judge)

evinces more true faith than could be shown by the most fluent religious conversation, the most intimate knowledge of Scripture doctrine, or the most remarkable agitation and change of religious sentiments. Yet how many are there who sit still with folded hands, dreaming, doing nothing at all, thinking they have done everything, or need do nothing, when they merely have had these good thoughts, which will save no one.[102]

In a sermon on the text 'Take ye heed, watch and pray; for ye know not when the time is' (Mark 13:33), Newman recognised there is often a reluctance to respond to God immediately:

Few will open to me immediately, when I knock. They will have something to do first; they will have to get ready. They will have to recover from the surprise and confusion which overtake them on the first news of My coming, and will need time to collect themselves, and summon about them their better thoughts and affections. They feel themselves very well off as they are; and wish to serve God as they are. They are satisfied to remain on earth; they do not wish to move; they do not wish to change.[103]

He therefore frequently appealed to his hearers and readers to respond to the call of God in their hearts and consciences; as he did, for example, on Ascension Day 1836:

Start, now, with this holy season, and rise with Christ. See, He offers you His hand; He is rising; rise with Him. Mount up from the grave of the old Adam; from grovelling cares, and jealousies, and fretfulness, and worldly aims; from the thraldom of habit, from the tumult of passion, from the fascinations of the flesh, from a cold, worldly, calculating spirit, from frivolity, from self-ishness ... Henceforth set about doing what it is so difficult to do, but what should not, must not be left undone; watch, and pray, and meditate, that is, according to the leisure which God has given you. Give freely of your time to your Lord and Saviour, if you have it. If you have little, show your sense of the privilege by giving that little ... Live more strictly to Him; take His yoke upon your shoulder; live by rule. I am not calling on you to go out of the world, or to abandon your duties in the world, but to redeem the time ... not altogether to omit to praise Him, or to intercede for the world and the Church; but in good measure to realise honestly the words of the text, to 'set your affection on things above'; and to prove that you are His, in that your heart is risen with Him, and your life hid in Him.[104]

In a sermon entitled 'The Eucharistic Presence' Newman urges:

Let us pray him to give us an earnest longing after him — a thirst for his presence — an anxiety to find him — a joy on hearing that he is to be found, even now, under the veil of sensible [i.e. known by the senses] things, —and a good hope that *we* shall find him there. Blessed indeed are they who have not seen, and yet have believed.[105]

People worry that they do not *feel* they love God: Newman gently suggests it is simply because they have not wished to love him, prayed to love him.

The one desire which should move us should be, first of all, that of seeing Him face to face, who is now hid from us; and next of enjoying eternal and direct communion, in and through Him, with our friends around us, whom at present we know only through the medium of sense, by precarious and partial channels, which give us little insight into their hearts.[106]

— 7 —

Cardinal John Henry Newman

NEWMAN'S WRITINGS, especially his *Apologia* (1864) and *Letter to the Duke of Norfolk* (1875) brought him immediate acclaim in both Churches and in public life. Ecumenically his importance lies in the fact that his journey from Anglicanism to Catholicism consisted of a long life of continual enrichment. He discovered the Catholic Faith for himself, not through Roman Catholicism as such or from Catholic priests, but from his own studies of the Scriptures and the Fathers. He famously wrote, 'Catholics did not make us Catholics; Oxford made us Catholics'.[1]

It was a day of unspeakable emotion and joy in 1878 when Newman was made the first honorary Fellow of his old college, Trinity, and he returned to Oxford for the first time since 1845. He called on Pusey, and saw the new college founded in memory of Keble, and went to Littlemore too. Next year came a letter from Rome. He had been made a Cardinal, the inestimable sign of approval from the earthly head of the Church. 'The cloud is lifted from me for ever', he cried. What Newman may not have realised is that had Manning still harboured any antipathy towards him he could have blocked it. The Duke of Norfolk and the Marquis of Ripon made an official request to Manning for him to raise Newman's elevation with the pope. When they did so, there was a long silence then the Cardinal bent his heard in thought and responded with the words of Mary: *Fiat voluntas Tua.*[2]

When news of his elevation broke it was deemed not just an honour on Newman, but an honour for England. The response from his fellow-country men to his *Apologia* had been remarkable and won him back many Anglican friends who had deserted him, but now he received a vast number of congratulations from Anglicans as well as Catholics. Octavius Ogle spoke for almost everyone when he wrote:

> I wonder if you know how much you are loved by England. I wonder if any man, at least in our time, was ever so loved by England — by all religiously minded England. And even the enemies of faith are softened by their feeling for you. And I

wonder whether this extraordinary and unparalleled love might not be—was not meant to be—utilised, as one means to draw together into one fold all Englishmen who believe.[3]

It was while he was in Rome to receive the formal message (*biglietto*) that Leo XIII was going to make him a cardinal that Newman, despite his age and frailty, stood to deliver a most remarkable discourse, which became known as the *Biglietto Speech*. So prophetic is it, so contemporary does it sound, that it is worth quoting at some length:

> For thirty, forty, fifty years I have resisted to the best of my powers the spirit of liberalism in religion ... Liberalism in religion is the doctrine that there is no positive truth in religion, but that one creed is as good as another, and this is the teaching which is gaining substance and force daily. It is inconsistent with any recognition of any religion, as true. It teaches that all are to be tolerated, for all are matters of opinion. Revealed religion is not a truth, but a sentiment and a taste; not an objective fact, not miraculous; and it is the right of each individual to make it say just what strikes his fancy ... Since, then, religion is so personal a peculiarity and so private a possession, we must of necessity ignore it in the intercourse of man with man. If a man puts on a new religion every morning, what is that to you? It is as impertinent to think about a man's religion as about his sources of income or his management of his family.

Religious liberalism leads to the privatisation of religion, and this in turn inevitably leads to secularism. Secularism, he saw immediately, would corrode community values and destroy the inner coherence of society, which had been formed by Christianity.

> Hitherto the civil Power has been Christian. Even in countries separated from the Church, as in my own, the dictum was in force, when I was young, that: 'Christianity was the law of the land'. Now, everywhere that goodly framework of society, which is the creation of Christianity, is throwing off Christianity ... Hitherto, it has been considered that religion alone, with its supernatural sanctions, was strong enough to secure submission of the masses of our population to law and order; now the Philosophers and Politicians are bent on satisfying this problem without the aid of Christianity. Instead of the Church's authority and teaching, they would substitute first of all a universal and a thoroughly secular education, calculated to bring home to every individual that to be orderly, industrious, and sober, is his personal interest ... As to Religion, it is a private luxury, which a man may have if he will; but which of course he must pay for, and which he must not obtrude upon others, or indulge in to their annoyance.

Infidelity is part of the reason for this state of affairs, but in England it arises particularly from the disunity of the different Christian denominations

> which sprang up in England three centuries ago, and which are so powerful now; [that] have ever been fiercely opposed to the union of Church and State, and would advocate the un-Christianising of the monarchy and all that belongs to it, under the notion that such a catastrophe would make Christianity much more pure and much more powerful.

Far from making Christianity more pure and powerful it only weakens the connection between Christianity and society, and causes the subject of religion to be ignored. Notwithstanding his sharp critique of liberalism in religion, Newman nonetheless recognises that the liberal and secular society is not without merit. Newman was insistent that there

> is much in the liberalistic theory which is good and true; for example, not to say more, the precepts of justice, truthfulness, sobriety, self-command, benevolence, which, as I have already noted, are among its avowed principles, and the natural laws of society. It is not till we find that this array of principles is intended to supersede, to block out, religion, that we pronounce it to be evil.

Modern liberal society has indeed in recent times produced beneficial laws against racism and other forms of discrimination. It has brought to public attention the needs of people with disabilities, and others who are disadvantaged. But as Newman predicted it seeks to supersede and block out Christianity and its influence in public affairs, The ills of society are frequently lamented today, but as Newman could foresee, 'the Philosophers and Politicians are bent on satisfying this problem without the aid of Christianity', and, he might have added, without success.

Newman ended his speech typically, with a paragraph of confidence and hope; grounded in his faith in the providence of God and the indwelling and guidance of the Holy Spirit in the Church. His knowledge of Church history and the remarkable and often unexpected way in which the Church is renewed from time to time, led him to this conviction:

> It must not be supposed for a moment that I am afraid of it. I lament it deeply, because I foresee that it may be the ruin of many souls; but I have no fear at all that it really can do aught of serious harm to the Word of God, to Holy Church, to our Almighty King, the Lion of the tribe of Judah, Faithful and True, or to His Vicar on earth. Christianity has been too often in what seemed deadly peril, that we should fear for it any new trial now. So far

is certain; on the other hand, what is uncertain, and in these great contests commonly is uncertain, and what is commonly a great surprise, when it is witnessed, is the particular mode by which, in the event, Providence rescues and saves His elect inheritance. Sometimes our enemy is turned into a friend; sometimes he is despoiled of that special virulence of evil which was so threatening; sometimes he falls to pieces of himself; sometimes he does just so much as is beneficial, and then is removed. Commonly the Church has nothing more to do than to go on in her own proper duties, in confidence and peace; to stand still and to see the salvation of God. 'The meek shall inherit the land and delight themselves in abundant peace' (Ps 37:11).[4]

He had written a similarly confident and prophetic paragraph in *The Church of the Fathers* in 1840:

The Church is ever militant. Sometimes she gains, sometimes she loses, and more often she is at once gaining and losing in different parts of her territory. Scarcely are we at peace when we are in persecution. Scarcely have we gained a triumph, when we are visited by a scandal. No, we make progress by means of reverses, our griefs are our consolations, we lose Stephen to gain Paul, and Matthias replaces the traitor Judas.[5]

— 8 —

Saint John Henry Newman

T HE CANONISATION OF NEWMAN was, of course, the Church's recognition and celebration of his sanctity: rather than his enormous
intellect and library of writings, or the prodigious influence his
thinking had and still has, in the Church. As well as his major works
we have a large collection of his poetry. An extraordinary twenty-one
thousand letters have survived; many of them, as King Charles III noted,
'not addressed to the fellow intellectuals and prominent leaders but
to family, friends and parishioners who sought out his wisdom'. His
personality lives in his letters, their style is conversational and even the
sound of his voice seems to be heard. His capacity for friendship was
immense. Throughout his lifetime Newman was revered, even back in
his Oxford days, and like saints through the ages he attracted 'disciples'
whom he led into deeper discipleship with the Lord. Undergraduates
would spot him in the street and whisper, 'There's Newman'. Once, in
his old age Newman heard that someone had referred to him as a saint,
and he wrote: 'I have no tendency to be a saint—it is a sad thing to say.
Saints are not literary men, they do not love the classics, they do not
write Tales [a reference to his two novels]. I may be well enough in my
way, but it is not the "high line". It is enough for me to black the saints'
shoes—if St. Philip uses blacking, in heaven.'[1]

But people recognise sanctity when they see it. John Coleridge, the
Lord Chief Justice, an Anglican, said of him in 1882,

> I cannot analyse it or explain it, but to this hour he interests and
> awes me like no other man I ever saw. He is simple and humble
> as a child, and, yet, I am with a being unlike anyone else. He
> lifts me up for the time, and subdues me—if I said frightens
> me it would hardly be too strong; and yet if he does this to a
> commonplace old lawyer, what must it be to men who can really
> enter into him and feel with him.[2]

In 1887, Bishop Ullathorne, soon to retire, visited him in the Oratory
House. Such was Newman's humility, even as a cardinal, that he knelt

to ask his blessing. Ullathorne wrote, 'I felt annihilated in his presence, there is a saint in that man'.[3]

As it is with saints so it was with Newman. The secret of his life was personal prayer, a theme that constantly occurred in his preaching and his letters, stirring up in others this desire which he had in himself. People sensed the man behind his words, and they had the witness of his life. He spent long hours in prayer every day, and kept notebooks of prayer from his Anglican days to the end of his life, praying still for the same people, in ever longer lists. Intercessory prayer was at the heart of Newman's understanding of priesthood both in his Anglican and his Catholic days. Jesus Christ is the mediator: he ever lives to intercede for us; and intercession is the priest's closest imitation of Christ. Intercession is 'characteristic of Christian worship, the privilege of heavenly adoption, the perfect and spiritual mind'. In a sermon on the privilege of Intercessory Prayer he preached:

> [Christ] died to bestow upon him that privilege which implies or involves all others, and brings him into nearest resemblance to Himself, the privilege of Intercession . . . He is made after the pattern and in the fullness of Christ—he is what Christ is. Christ intercedes above, and he intercedes below.[4]

He prayed for others and he also prayed for himself, as his notebooks show. He prayed *for* things and *against* things. On Fridays for instance he prayed, among other things, for 'zeal, singleness of heart, simple dependence on the grace of Christ, regarding myself as an *instrument*, for liveliness and fervency of prayer, for a deep sense of the awful nature of my sacred office, regarding myself as the voice of the people to God, and of God to the people, for the spirit of devotion, affection towards my people—love, fear, confidence towards God . . . for strength of body, nerves, voice, breath & earnestness of manner, distinctiveness of delivery'. Asking for 'fervour' was a frequent request. In *Meditations and Devotions* that were assembled shortly after his death, he explained in a prayer:

> Lord, in asking for fervour, I am asking for Thyself . . . Thou art the living Flame . . . enter into me and set me on fire after Thy pattern and likeness.

A prayer he wrote for his First Communion as an Anglican in Trinity College Chapel when he was sixteen, he re-copied many times, and used even as a Cardinal of the Catholic Church.

> Lord I praise Thee for calling me to the light of Thy Gospel—for my birth in a country where Thy true religion is found, and for Thy goodness in enlightening my soul with the knowledge of Thy Truth, that, whereas I was proud, self-righteous, impure,

abominable, Thou wast pleased to turn me from such a state of darkness and irreligion, by a mercy which is too wonderful for me, and make me fall down humbled and abased before Thy footstool. O let me so run the race that is set before me that I may lay hold of everlasting life, and especially let me make Thee, O Holy Jesus, my pattern in my pilgrimage here, that Thou mayest be the portion of my soul to all eternity.[5]

Within the covers of this private notebook are prayers written by a boy of sixteen, the young Anglican deacon of twenty-three, and the Oratorian Cardinal when he was eighty-eight; a wonderful continuity of prayers. In another notebook he used each day before Mass are the names of people he prayed for regularly, listed under headings which include 'Auld Lang Syne', 'Protestants', 'those dear to me', 'kind to me', 'cold to me', 'no how to me', 'godchildren', 'cousins', 'St Mary's and Littlemore', 'faithful women', 'those with claim on me', 'loyal to me', 'Catholics 1', Catholics 2 and Catholics 3', 'Irish friends', 'for the Oratory', 'Ecclesiastical', 'Converts', 'the Dead'.

Apart from the innumerable actual prayers he wrote, his hymns and poems were also prayers, the most memorable being, perhaps, 'Praise to the Holiest in the Height', part of his incomparable *Dream of Gerontius*. When William Gladstone lay dying he frequently quoted this hymn, a comforting solace in his last days. Newman wrote and preached from what he experienced in the depths of his being through prayer, and people knew this. No one who has read and used the collection of *Meditations and Devotions* could doubt this for a moment. One, who as a boy knew him at the Oratory, was Edward Burne-Jones, who later in life recalled Newman's influence upon him.

> When I was fifteen or sixteen he taught me so much ... things that will never be out of me. In an age of sofas and cushions he taught me to be indifferent to comfort; and in an age of materialism he taught me to venture all on the unseen ... so that if this world cannot tempt me with money and luxury, and it can't, or honours of anything else in its trumpery treasure house it is most of all because he said it to me in a way that touched me—not scolding nor forbidding nor much leaning—walking with me a step in front.[6]

Newman spoke frequently of holiness, and the perseverance and discipline needed to find it. Like those who heard him, as we read his words on the saints, it is difficult to escape the conclusion that, though he would never be aware of it, he was speaking of himself. The saints

> have attained such noble self-command, they have so crucified the flesh, they have so renounced the world; they are so meek,

so gentle, so tender-hearted, so merciful, so sweet, so cheerful, so full of prayer, so diligent, so forgetful of injuries; they have sustained such great and continued pains, they have persevered in such vast labours, they have made such valiant confessions, they have wrought such abundant miracles, they have been blessed with such strange successes, that they have set up a standard before us of truth, of magnanimity, of holiness, of love.[7]

Newman's whole life, his purpose, his desires, his decisions, were centred on his love for Jesus Christ. And his beliefs and teaching were so grounded in the Gospel and the teachings of the apostles that their words became his own:

What gain is it to please the world, to please the great, nay even to please those whom we love, compared with this? What gain is it to be applauded, admired, courted, followed — compared with this one aim, of not being 'disobedient to a heavenly vision'? What can this world offer comparable with that insight into spiritual things, that keen faith, that heavenly peace, that high sanctity, that everlasting righteousness, that hope of glory, which they have, who in sincerity love and follow our Lord Jesus Christ? Let us beg and pray Him day by day to reveal Himself to our souls more fully, to quicken our senses, to give us sight and hearing, taste and touch of the world to come; so to work within us, that we may sincerely say, 'Thou shall guide me with Thy counsel, and after that receive me with glory. Whom have I in heaven but Thee? and there is none upon earth that I desire in comparison of Thee. My flesh and my heart faileth, but God is the strength of my heart, and my portion for ever.'[8]

He gave his soul back to God on 11 August 1890 in his ninetieth year. He had lived eleven years after being made a Cardinal: years that he continued to devote to praying, writing, preaching when he could, and in leading his growing community and thriving school; keeping up, as ever, with his correspondence and meeting all who came to see him. He fell several times, his eyesight deteriorated and he had to dictate his letters. But they were years of contentment, free from the setbacks, controversies and misunderstandings, which had, for him, been a means of grace, borne without complaint. Cardinal Hume remarked: 'Let me be quite clear. A holy person is canonised only if he or she gives evidence of heroic sanctity ... Does [Newman] bear the mark of the undoubted saint? I believe we may underestimate what it must have cost him to struggle faithfully to the end.'

The Oratory was filled for his Funeral Mass with bishops, hundreds of Catholic clergy and dignitaries, his pupils from the Oratory School, the Duke of Norfolk, the Lord Chief Justice, Anglican clergy and Oxford dons. And more than 15,000 of the poor people of Birmingham to whom he had devoted his life lined the route from the Oratory to Rednal, where he, one of England's greatest sons, was laid to rest.

Tributes came not only from Catholics everywhere, and in all the newspapers, including Jewish ones; from the sporting fraternity (though Newman was never a sportsman); from Anglicans describing what he had done for their Church, and what he had done in England to break down hatred of Catholicism, as well as from countless known and unknown individuals. Jane Todd, a seamstress from Scarborough, said he 'carried through labours and fatigues of mind and body by the vision of the unseen'. Eleanor Watts hoped, 'Please God my prayers may be answered that I shall live to see his canonisation begin before I die. He has certainly been canonised by the voice of the people'.[9]

Popular acclamation would indeed have been sufficient for his canonisation in the early centuries, but for someone to be proposed as a model and intercessor for the faithful, the Church now looks for evidence of heroic virtue and fidelity to God's grace in their life, and also the efficacy of their prayers with the Lord after death. The miracle chosen for the beatification of John Henry Newman was the medically inexplicable healing of John Sullivan, a man from Boston, who was studying for the permanent diaconate. He suffered from a back condition and underwent spinal surgery on 15 August 2001, but the surgeons unfortunately encountered serious complications including the tearing of the *dura mater* (the membrane round the spine). He was left in excruciating pain and was told he was on the brink of complete paralysis. A few days later, unable to get out of bed, he prayed, 'Please Cardinal Newman, help me to walk, so that I can return to classes and be ordained'.

> As soon as I had finished making this prayer I felt a tremendous sensation of intense heat all over, and a strong tingling feeling throughout my body. This feeling of heat and tingling seemed to last a long time! In addition I felt an indescribable sense of joy and peace, as though in the presence of God. I also had a renewed sense of hope and confidence that finally, I could walk! When this beautiful moment subsided, I realized, much to my surprise, I was standing upright. I said to the nurse: 'I have no more pain,' whereas minutes before, I was bent over in complete agony. During these precious moments, I was totally captivated, totally transfixed by God's loving presence! I realized that I could walk pain free, when I couldn't for months. I could walk upright. I could walk with strength in my back and in my legs!
>
> I was so totally invigorated that I sprinted out of my room and then up and down all the corridors on my floor of the hospital. The poor nurse tagging behind kept shouting 'Jack slow

down—slow down!' Immediately thereafter, I was discharged, and to everyone's astonishment I returned to my classes on time!

His surgeon confirmed:

> Your recovery is unbelievable, 100 per cent and totally remarkable. I have never seen a healing process occur so quickly and so completely ... I have absolutely no medical explanation to give you as to why your pain stopped. The MRI scans and the subsequent intrusive surgery confirmed the severity of your spinal condition. With the tear in your *dura mater* your condition should have been much worse. I have no medical or scientific explanation for you. If you want an answer, ask God.

A year later, on 14 September 2002, the Feast of the Triumph of the Holy Cross, he was ordained a deacon at the Cathedral of the Holy Cross in Boston. Without knowing the date of his ordination, on that self-same day, the Postulator for Newman's cause notified him, that 'the Fathers at the Birmingham Oratory had voted to formally initiate the process for the beatification of their founder, the Venerable John Henry Cardinal Newman, and to take his case to Rome'. Ten years later, after the usual investigations, including examination of all the medical evidence, Newman was beatified in Birmingham by Pope Benedict XVI on 19 September 2010. In his homily, the Pope said:

> Cardinal Newman's motto, *Cor ad cor loquitur*, or 'Heart speaks unto heart', gives us an insight into his understanding of the Christian life as a call to holiness, experienced as the profound desire of the human heart to enter into intimate communion with the Heart of God. He reminds us that faithfulness to prayer gradually transforms us into the divine likeness. As he wrote in one of his many fine sermons, 'a habit of prayer, the practice of turning to God and the unseen world in every season, in every place, in every emergency—prayer, I say, has what may be called a natural effect in spiritualising and elevating the soul. A man is no longer what he was before; gradually ... he has imbibed a new set of ideas, and become imbued with fresh principles'.

Benedict XVI concluded his homily with some thoughts on Newman's ministry as a pastor:

> The warmth and humanity underlying his appreciation of the pastoral ministry is beautifully expressed in [one] of his ...sermons: 'Had Angels been your priests, my brethren, they could not have condoled with you, sympathised with you, have had compassion on you, felt tenderly for you, and made allowances for you, as we can; they could not have been your patterns and guides, and have led you on from your old selves into a new

life, as they can who come from the midst of you'. He lived out that profoundly human vision of priestly ministry in his devoted care for the people of Birmingham during the years that he spent at the Oratory he founded, visiting the sick and the poor, comforting the bereaved, caring for those in prison. No wonder that on his death so many thousands of people lined the local streets as his body was taken to its place of burial not half a mile from here. One hundred and twenty years later, great crowds have assembled once again to rejoice in the Church's solemn recognition of the outstanding holiness of this much-loved father of souls. Such spiritual fathers and mothers are sorely needed in today's Church.

Let Deacon Sullivan have the last word. 'Since [the miracle] Newman has become a significant part of my life . . . I have developed a very real relationship with Cardinal Newman in frequent prayer and I try to pass on what marvellous gifts I have received to those I meet'.

The second miracle accepted for Newman's canonisation was the healing of Melissa Villalobos from the Archdiocese of Chicago, a law graduate, then a mother of four. Confirmed as pregnant in April 2013, on 1 May she began to bleed heavily, and this became worse over the next days. On 10 May a sub-chorionic haematoma, a blood clot caused by a partially detached (or ripped) placenta, on the foetal membrane, was diagnosed. By then it was three times the size of the child. There was no treatment, and her doctors expected her to miscarry, warning her that she could haemorrhage seriously and that if that happened her life would be in grave danger without immediate medical treatment.

Bed rest was ordered for a lengthy period, not easy for a mother with children aged 6, 5, 3 and 18 months. The bleeding increased each day, along with cramping, until on 15 May she found herself on the bathroom floor with blood haemorrhaging alarmingly, with only the children in the house, downstairs. In that life-threatening situation she begged aloud 'Please Cardinal Newman make the bleeding stop!' Instantly it did so, going from a very heavy flow to a complete stop as if a rushing hose was immediately shut off. This was followed by a sudden burst of fragrant roses which filled the air, and she knew then that she had been healed. 'It was more intense than if you were in a garden, or a store and smelled roses. I inhaled the smell of the roses and thought "Wow!".' Hardly able to believe it she asked 'Cardinal Newman did you make those roses for me?' Then a second blast came and 'I realised I was OK and the baby was OK'. She got up, went downstairs and sat in the kitchen and said 'Thank you Cardinal Newman'. And the scent came a third time filling the kitchen. Melissa was taken to hospital. An ultrasound scan revealed that the placenta had healed perfectly. Nor—to the astonishment of doctors, some of whom later gave evidence to the Church investigation into the healing—was there any trace of the haematoma. Her pregnancy progressed normally and she gave birth to Gemma.

All she knew of Newman was from a television programme she had just seen. This was what made her cry to him for help. She is now an eager reader of Newman's works, especially his letters 'because they reveal Newman's care for ordinary people', she said: 'He is like a spiritual father to me. He is a guiding light to help me live a holier life and to learn about the Faith. He explains Jesus in a way that is simple and profound . . . he helps me to know Jesus more accurately'.

And this, of course, is what the saints do, by their lives, by their teaching, and by their prayers.

John Henry Cardinal Newman, pray for us to the Lord.

$\sim$ 9 $\sim$

Doctor of the Church

AT HIS CANONISATION voices were heard calling for Newman to be declared a Doctor of the Church. The bishops of England and Wales, Scotland and Ireland, as well as the bishops of the United States added their weight, as did academic institutions, religious orders and ecclesial communities and others from around the world; making it clear that there was a growing consensus in the universal Church. Pope Benedict XVI had concluded a lecture with the words:

> The characteristic of the great Doctor of the Church, it seems to me, is that he teaches not only through his thought and speech, but rather by his life, because within him thought and life are interpenetrated and defined. If this is so, then Newman belongs to the great teachers of the Church, because at the same time he touches our hearts and enlightens our thinking.[1]

Shortly before he died, Pope Benedict said: 'Newman—Doctor of the Church, that would be a light for the darkness of this time!'

On 31 July 2025 Pope Leo XIV confirmed the affirmative opinion of the Plenary Session of Cardinals and Bishops, members of the Dicastery for the Causes of Saints, that the title of Doctor of the Universal Church, would soon be conferred on Saint John Henry Newman. The news was greeted with joy. Lord Mendoza, the Provost of Newman's old college in Oxford was delighted by the announcement, paying tribute to the 'profound impact Newman made as a Fellow of Oriel College from 1822 until 1845, on the study of theology, on the university and on daily academic life here and across Oxford'. The Archbishop of Westminster, Cardinal Vincent Nichols, said: 'This recognition that the writings of St John Henry Newman are a true expression of the faith of the Church is of huge encouragement to all who appreciate not only his great learning but also his heroic sanctity in following the call of God'. Speaking for the Church of England, the Archbishop of York, Dr Stephen Cottrell welcomed the news, saying that Newman was a 'profound teacher both to Anglicans and Catholics, a spiritual guide, and model of holiness'.

As others have noted, the fact that Newman's teachings are recognised as completely orthodox is remarkable since much of his output was produced in his Anglican days.

The significance of saints being declared Doctors of the Church is the recognition by the Church of the depth of their understanding of the Faith, and the orthodoxy and truth of their teaching and writing. They have made an exceptional contribution to theology and the formulation of Christian Faith; they are reliable witness to the Faith and therefore of great relevance to the Church, not only in their own day but for the future. The prophetic Newman is a guide for our times, not least in his insistence on the vital need for every human being to obey their conscience (listening to the voice of God); and for the New Evangelisation, with his teaching on consulting the faithful laity, and his emphasis on the heart, and on prayer and seeking holiness. He held fast to dogma and the reality of Divine Revelation, the authority and necessity of the One Catholic Church and of being in communion with the successor of St Peter, while at the same time recognising the way in which the Faith deepens and develops through ongoing reflection under the guidance of the Holy Spirit of Truth.

The Bishops' Conference of England and Wales explained that the Church gives 'the title "Doctor", from the Latin *docere* meaning "to teach"',

> because she recognises that each of them has made an outstanding, or 'eminent' contribution to our knowledge of the faith—whether in its spiritual, intellectual or moral dimensions ... for more than a century [Newman's] teaching has been valued for all these qualities that characterise a Doctor of the Church. Newman's teaching has been acclaimed by many popes, from Leo XIII to Leo XIV, including Pope St Pius X, Pope Pius XI, Pope Ven. Pius XII, Pope St John XXIII, Pope St Paul VI, Pope St John Paul II, Pope Benedict XVI and Pope Francis. While many Doctors of the Church are notable for one particular aspect of their teaching, St John Henry Newman is especially remarkable for the breadth of his teaching across many aspects of the faith, his influence upon various branches of doctrine and theology, and his engagement with problems of faith which remain burning issues in our own time.

Doctors of the Church are all canonised saints, men and women of great holiness as well as great learning, saints who continue to speak to the Church today, despite the passage of time and the social and cultural boundaries that divide us from them, because of their own faithful discipleship, and responsiveness to the Holy Spirit.

Very few people have been given this title. Newman becomes only the 38th Doctor of the Church, and they include such giants and luminaries as Ss Gregory the Great, Augustine, Thomas Aquinas and Teresa of Avila: he is the second English person, along with the Venerable Bede (d. 735). One other associated with England was the Italian-born St Anselm, Archbishop of Canterbury (d. 1109). England, indeed the world, is greatly blessed to have the light of his presence in Christ and his teaching to guide us today.

10

Hymns

Lead Kindly Light

WRITTEN AS A POEM entitled 'The Pillar and the Cloud' in 1833 when Newman was travelling in Italy, ill and homesick, Newman explained:

Before starting from my inn in the morning of May 26th or 27th, I sat down on my bed and began to sob violently . . . I was aching to get home, yet for want of a vessel I was kept at Palermo for three weeks. I began to visit the churches, and they calmed my impatience, though I did not attend any services . . . At last I got off in an orange boat, bound for Marseilles. We were becalmed for whole week in the Straits of Bonifacio. Then it was that I wrote the lines, *Lead, Kindly Light*, which have since become well known. I was writing verses the whole time of my passage.

Famously, it was sung by miners trapped underground in the terrible Durham mining disaster of 1909. *The night is dark, and I am far away from home.* It was sung by Betsie ten Boom, sister of Corrie ten Boom, and other women as they were led to the concentration camp of Ravensbrück during the Holocaust. It was being sung by a soloist, Marion Wright, on the *RMS Titanic* shortly before she struck an iceberg on 14 April 1912, and was sung on one of the lifeboats when the rescue ship *RMS Carpathia* was spotted. It was also sung by British troops during the First World War at Services held before going into the trenches.

> Lead, Kindly Light, amidst th' encircling gloom,
>   Lead Thou me on!
> The night is dark, and I am far from home,
>   Lead Thou me on!
> Keep Thou my feet; I do not ask to see
> The distant scene; one step enough for me.
>
> I was not ever thus, nor prayed that Thou
>   Shouldst lead me on;

I loved to choose and see my path; but now
   Lead Thou me on!
I loved the garish day, and, spite of fears,
Pride ruled my will. Remember not past years!

So long Thy power hath blest me, sure it still
   Will lead me on.
O'er moor and fen, o'er crag and torrent, till
   The night is gone,
And with the morn those angel faces smile,
Which I have loved long since, and lost awhile!

The Dream of Gerontius

'Firmly I Believe and truly' and 'Praise to the Holiest' are found in the beautiful, epic poem, the *Dream of Gerontius*. Written in 1865, the poem describes the passage of Gerontius (lit. 'an old man') through death; a lesson in how to meet death. Newman told a friend afterwards, 'It came into my head to write it, I really can't tell how. And I wrote it until it was finished, on small bits of paper, and I could no more write anything else by willing it than I could fly'. His understanding of Purgatory as a personal encounter with God, rather than of punishment by fire, was unusual then in Catholic theology, but Newman argued that the received teaching of purgation by fire was no longer used in the definition of the doctrine at the Council of Trent. The *Dream* was acclaimed, reprinted numerous times and translated into French and German. Edward Elgar had long thought about setting it to music, and achieved his hopes for the Birmingham Music Festival of 1900. He said 'It is the best of me', and many agree it his finest work.

The dying and faithful Gerontius is surrounded by a priest and his friends who are praying with him, and invoking the saints in litanies and prayers. He is fearful but confident. And he makes a magnificent and impassioned act of faith, 'Firmly I Believe and truly', as death approaches.

Firmly I believe and truly
God is Three and God is One;
and I next acknowledge duly
manhood taken by the Son

And I trust and hope most fully
in that manhood crucified;
and each thought and deed unruly
do to death, as he has died.

Simply to his grace and wholly
light and life and strength belong,

and I love supremely, solely,
him the holy, him the strong.

And I hold in veneration,
for the love of him alone,
Holy Church as his creation,
and her teachings as his own.

Adoration ay be given,
with and through the angelic host,
to the God of earth and heaven,
Father, Son, and Holy Ghost.

He hears the priest intoning the Church's Prayers for the dying: 'Go forth upon thy journey, Christian soul! Go from this world! Go, in the Name of God the Omnipotent Father, who created thee! Go, in the Name of Jesus Christ, our Lord, Son of the living God, who bled for thee! Go, in the Name of the Holy Spirit, who Hath been pour'd out on thee!'

Soon Gerontius falls asleep in death, and then reawakens as a soul, preparing for judgement. He is just aware of the priest saying the prayers after death, the *Subvenite*: 'Saints of God come to his aid! Come to meet him, angels of the Lord'. Now he becomes aware of his Guardian Angel accompanying him and explaining what is happening to him. 'For thee bitterness of death is passed . . . because already in thy soul the judgement is begun.' They safely pass a group of demons: 'How impotent they are! and yet on earth they have repute for wondrous power and skill.'

Five choirs of what Newman calls 'Angelicals' sing out, as the King puts it, in 'a grand mysterious harmony' eternally praising God for His grace and forgiveness. Four versions of 'Praise to the Holiest' culminate in the verses of the 'Song of Christ's Redemption' we know best:

Praise to the Holiest in the height
And in the depth be praise:
In all His words most wonderful;
Most sure in all His ways!

O loving wisdom of our God!
When all was sin and shame,
A second Adam to the fight
And to the rescue came.

O wisest love! that flesh and blood
Which did in Adam fail,
Should strive afresh against the foe,
Should strive and should prevail;

And that a higher gift than grace
Should flesh and blood refine,

God's Presence and His very Self,
And Essence all divine.

O gen'rous love! that He who smote
In man for man the foe,
The double agony in man
For man should undergo;

And in the garden secretly,
And on the cross on high,
Should teach His brethren and inspire
To suffer and to die.

Praise to the Holiest in the height
And in the depth be praise:
In all His words most wonderful;
Most sure in all His ways!

Finally, Gerontius glimpses God and is judged in a single moment. The Guardian Angel speaks:

Softly and gently, dearly-ransom'd soul,
in my most loving arms I now enfold thee

and lowers Gerontius into the waters of Purgatory, with a final blessing and the promise of a re-awakening to glory.

Farewell, but not for ever! brother dear; Be brave and patient on thy bed of sorrow; Swiftly shall pass thy night of trial here, And I will come and wake thee on the morrow. Farewell! Farewell! And Masses on the earth, and prayers in heaven, shall aid thee at the Throne of the Most Highest.

— 11 —

Personal Prayers

Morning Prayer
(written when he was sixteen)

God Almighty! Keep me through this day! Let me grow in grace! Thou, O God! have graciously brought me to the beginning of this day, defend me in the same by thy mighty power! Grant, O Lord, that as I now arise this morning after sleep, fresh, healthful, and rejoicing, so my body, after the sleep of death, may rise, spiritualised and blessed to dwell with Thee for evermore!

A Daily Prayer

May He support us all the day long, till the shades lengthen and the evening comes, and the busy world is hushed, and the fever of life is over, and our work is done. Then in His mercy may He give us a safe lodging, and a holy rest and peace at the last.

A Prayer of Trust

God has created me to do Him some definite service;
He has committed some work to me, which He has not committed to
    another.
I have my mission—I may never know it in this life, but I shall be told
    it in the next . . .
I am a link in a chain, a bond of connection between persons.
He has not created me for naught. I shall do good, I shall do His work;
I shall be an angel of peace, a preacher of truth in my own place, while
    not intending it,
if I do but keep His commandments and serve Him in my calling.
Therefore I will trust Him.
Whatever, wherever I am, I can never be thrown away.

If I am in sickness, my sickness may serve Him;
In perplexity, my perplexity may serve Him;
If I am in sorrow, my sorrow may serve Him ...
He may prolong my life, He may shorten it;
He knows what He is about.
He may take away my friends; He may throw me among strangers,
He may make me feel desolate, make my spirits sink
Hide the future from me—still He knows what He is about.

O Adonai, O Ruler of Israel,
Thou that guidest Joseph like a flock,
O Emmanuel, O Sapientia,
I give myself to Thee. I trust Thee wholly.
Thou art wiser than I—more loving than I myself.
Deign to fulfil Thy high purposes in me whatever they be—work in
    and through me.
I am born to serve Thee, to be Thy instrument.
Let me be Thy blind instrument.
I ask not to see—ask not to know—I ask simply to be used.

A Prayer in God's Grace

O my Lord Jesus, low as I am in Thy all holy sight, I am strong in Thee,
strong through Thy Immaculate Mother, through Thy saints and thus
I can do much for the Church, for the world, for all I love.

Learning Christ

Teach me, my Lord, to be sweet and gentle in all the events of life: in
disappointments, in the thoughtlessness of others, in the insincerity
of those I trusted, in the unfaithfulness of those on whom I relied.
Let me put myself aside, to think of the happiness of others, to hide
my little pains and heartaches, so that I may be the only one to suffer
them. Teach me to profit by the suffering that comes across my path.
Let me so use it that it may mellow me, not harden nor embitter me;
that it may make me patient, not irritable, that it may make me broad
in my forgiveness, not narrow, haughty and overbearing. May no one
be less good for having come within my influence. No one less pure,
less noble for having been a fellow-traveller in our journey toward
eternal life. As I go my rounds from one distraction to another, let me
whisper, from time to time, a word of love to You. May our life be lived
in the supernatural, full of power for good, and strong in its purpose
of sanctity. Amen.

Radiating Christ

Dear Jesus, help me to spread Thy fragrance everywhere I go. Flood my soul with Thy spirit and life. Penetrate and possess my whole being so utterly that all my life may only be a radiance of Thine. Shine through me and be so in me that every soul I come in contact with may feel Thy presence in my soul. Let them look up and see no longer me but only Jesus! Stay with me and then I shall begin to shine as Thou shinest, so to shine as to be a light to others; the light, O Jesus, will be all from Thee; none of it will be mine: it will be Thee shining on others through me. Let me thus praise Thee in the way Thou lovest best: by shining on those around me. Let me preach Thee without preaching, not by words, but by my example, by the catching force, the sympathetic influence of what I do, the evident fullness of the love my heart bears to Thee.

Prayer to Our Lady

O Mother of Jesus, and my Mother, let me dwell with thee, cling to thee and love thee with ever–increasing love. I promise the honour, love and trust of a child. Give me a mother's protection, for I need thy watchful care. You know better than any other the thoughts and desires of the Sacred Heart. Keep constantly before my mind the same thoughts, the same desires, that my heart may be filled with zeal for the interests of the Sacred Heart of thy Divine Son. Instil in me a love of all that is noble, that I may no longer be easily turned to selfishness. Help me, dearest Mother, to acquire the virtues that God wants of me: to forget myself always, to work solely for him, without fear of sacrifice. I shall always rely on thy help to be what Jesus wants me to be. I am his; I am thine, my good Mother! Give me each day thy holy and maternal blessing until my last evening on earth, when thy Immaculate Heart will present me to the heart of Jesus in heaven, there to love and bless thee and thy divine Son for all eternity.

Candlemas

And while the sword in Mary's soul
Is driven home, we hide
In our own hearts, and count the wounds
Of passion and of pride
And still, though Candlemas be spent
And Alleluias o'er
Mary is music in our needs,
And Jesus light in store.

Prayer to the Holy Spirit, the Life of the Church

I adore Thee, O my Lord, the Third Person of the All-Blessed Trinity, that Thou hast set up in this world of sin a great light upon a hill. Thou hast founded the Church, Thou hast established and maintained it. Thou fillest it continually with Thy gifts, that men may see, and draw near, and take, and live. Thou hast in this way brought down heaven upon earth. For Thou hast set up a great company which Angels visit by that ladder which the patriarch saw in vision. Thou hast by Thy presence restored the communion between God above and man below. Thou hast given him that light of grace which is one with and the commencement of the light in glory. I adore and praise Thee for Thy infinite mercy towards us, O my Lord and God.

Prayer for Salvation

God, who for the redemption of the world wast pleased to be born; to be circumcised; to be rejected; to be betrayed; to be bound with thongs; to be led to the slaughter; to be shamefully gazed at; to be falsely accused; to be scourged and torn; to be spit upon, and crowned with thorns; to be mocked and reviled; to be buffeted and struck with rods; to be stripped; to be nailed to the cross; to be hoisted up thereon; to be reckoned among thieves; to have gall and vinegar to drink; to be pierced with a lance: through Thy most holy passion, which we, Thy sinful servants, call to mind, and by Thy holy cross and gracious death, deliver us from the pains of hell, and lead us whither Thou didst lead the thief who was crucified with Thee, who with the Father and the Holy Ghost livest and reignest, God, world without end. Amen.

Prayer before the Cross

God, Who by the Precious Blood of Thy only-begotten Son didst sanctify the standard of the Cross, grant, we beseech Thee, that we who rejoice in the glory of the same Cross may at all times and places rejoice in Thy protection, through the same Christ, our Lord.

Prayer before Holy Communion

My God, enable me to bear Thee, for Thou alone canst. Cleanse my heart and mind from all that is past. Wipe out clean all my recollections of evil. Rid me from all languor, sickliness, irritability, feebleness of soul. Give me a true perception of things unseen, and make me truly, practically, and in the details of life, prefer Thee to anything on earth, and the future world to the present. Give me courage, a true instinct determining between right and wrong, humility in all things, and a tender longing love of Thee.

Prayer before the Blessed Sacrament

I place myself in the presence of Him, in whose Incarnate Presence I am before I place myself there. I adore You, O my Saviour, present here as God and Man, in Soul and Body, in true Flesh and Blood. I acknowledge and confess that I kneel before the Sacred Humanity, which was conceived in Mary's womb, and lay in Mary's bosom; which grew up to man's estate, and by the Sea of Galilee called the Twelve, wrought miracles, and spoke words of wisdom and peace; which in due season hung on the cross, lay in the tomb, rose from the dead, and now reigns in heaven. I praise and bless, and give myself wholly to Him, Who is the true Bread of my soul, and my everlasting joy. Amen.

Prayer for a Happy Death

Oh, my Lord and Saviour, support me in that hour in the strong arms of Thy Sacraments, and by the fresh fragrance of Thy consolations. Let the absolving words be said over me, and the holy oil sign and seal me, and Thine own Body be my food, and Thy Blood my sprinkling; and let my sweet Mother, Mary, breathe on me, and my Angel whisper peace to me, and my glorious Saints smile upon me; that in them all, and through them all, I may receive the gift of perseverance, and die, as I desire to live, in Thy faith, in Thy Church, in Thy service, and in Thy love. Amen.

Prayer on Christ's Ascension

O Emmanuel! O God in our flesh! we too hope, by Thy grace, to follow Thee. We will cling to the skirts of Thy garments, as Thou goest up; for without Thee we cannot ascend. O Emmanuel, what a day of joy when we shall enter heaven! O inexpressible ecstasy, after all the trouble! There is none but Thou. 'Thou hast held me by Thy right hand; and by Thy will Thou hast conducted me, and with Thy glory Thou hast received me. For what have I in heaven? And besides Thee what do I desire upon earth? For Thee my flesh and my heart hath fainted away: Thou art the God of my heart, and the God of my portion for ever.'

Catholic Collect
for St John Henry Newman's Feast Day, 9 October

O God, who bestowed on your Priest Saint John Henry Newman the grace to follow your kindly light and find peace in your Church; graciously grant that, through his intercession and example, we may be led out of shadows and images into the fullness of your truth. Through our Lord Jesus Christ, your Son, who lives and reigns with you in the unity of the Holy Spirit, God, for ever and ever. Amen.

Anglican Collect
for John Henry Newman's Feast Day, 11 August

God of all wisdom, we thank you for John Henry Newman, whose eloquence bore witness that your Church is one, holy, catholic and apostolic, and who made his own life a pilgrimage towards your truth. Grant that, inspired by his words and example, we may ever follow your kindly light till we rest in your bosom, with your dear Son Jesus Christ and the Holy Spirit, where heart speaks to heart eternally; for you live and reign, one God, now and for ever. Amen.

NOTES

Chapter 1

1   J. H. Newman, *Apologia pro Vita Sua* (London, 1994), p. 28.

2   *The Letters and Diaries of John Henry Newman*, ed. C. S. Dessain (London, 1963), vol. XXXI, p. 189.

3   J. H. Newman, *Letters and Correspondence of John Henry Newman*, ed. Anne Mozley (London, 1891), vol. I, ch. 3, *Autobiographical Memoir* (New York, 1957), p. 122.

4   *Apologia*, pp. 27–8.

Chapter 2

1   J. H. Newman, *Autobiographical Writings*, ed. H. Tristram (London, 1956), p. 200.

2   J. H. Newman, 'On the Nature of the Future Promise, A Sermon at St Clement's', ed. Attilio Rossi, *Newman Studies Journal* 10/2 (2013), pp. 74–87.

3   *Apologia*, p. 41.

4   J. H. Newman, *Parochial and Plain Sermons* (San Francisco, 1987), vol. II, Sermon 12, p. 309.

5   *Vatican Council II*, vol. I, ed. A. Flannery (Leominster, 1992), *Dogmatic Constitution on Divine Revelation (Dei Verbum)*, para. 5, p. 752.

6   *Parochial and Plain Sermons*, vol. V, Sermon 16, p. 1093.

7   *Ibid.*, Sermon 17, pp. 1102–3.

8   R. W. Church, *The Oxford Movement: 1833–1845* (London, 1891), p. 130.

9   W. Lockhart, *Cardinal Newman: A Retrospect of Fifty Years, by one of his oldest living disciples* (London, 1891), pp. 25–6).

10   Cited in E. Short, *Newman and his Contemporaries* (London, 2011), p. 3.

11   J. A. Froude, *Short Studies of Great Subjects* (London, 1917), vol. IV, pp. 283–4.

12   *Ibid.*, p. 286.

13   D. P. Deavel, 'Iron Hardness, Surpassing Sweetness: Newman as Preacher', *Logos: A Journal of Catholic Thought and Culture* 14/4 (2011), pp. 177–8.

14   *Parochial and Plain Sermons*, vol. VI, Sermon 15, p. 1309.

15   Cited in C. S. Dessain, *John Henry Newman* (London, 1966), p. 44.

16   J. H. Newman, *Sermons bearing upon Subjects of the Day* (London, 1885), Sermon XIX, pp. 286–7.

17   J. H. Newman, *Letter to the Duke of Norfolk* (London, 2015), Section 2, 'The Ancient Church', p. 13.

Chapter 3

1   Ecclesiastical Commissioners for England Archive Collection, https://archive-shub.jisc.ac.uk/search/locations/48937fab-b013-39c0-a2fb-b4f0f7c78a34, Ref. GB 109.

2   J. H. Newman, *Sermons on Subjects of the Day* (London, 1885), Sermon 26, p. 409.

3   J. H. Newman, *Discourses Addressed to Mixed Congregations* (Waterford, 2018), p. 5.

4   J. H. Newman, *An Essay on the Development of Christian Doctrine* (Notre Dame, Indiana, 1994), p. 14.

5   *Ibid.*, p. 30.

6   *Ibid.*, p. 45.

7   *Ibid.*, p. 47.

8   *Apologia*, p. 200.

9   *Ibid.*, p. 206.

10   *Ibid.*, p. 208.

11   J. H. Newman, *Sermons Preached on Various Occasions* (London, 1908), Sermon X, pp. 171–2.

Chapter 4

1   J. H. Newman, *Difficulties Felt by Anglicans in Catholic Teaching* (London, 1908), vol. I, Lecture 4, p. 98.

2   Cited in Dessain, *John Henry Newman*, p. 85.

3   *Difficulties*, vol. I, Lecture 1, p. 4.

4   *Ibid.*, Lecture 12, pp. 367–8.

5   *Ibid.*, Lecture 4, pp. 124–5.

6   *Letters and Diaries*, vol. XI, p. 14.

7   *Ibid.*, vol. XIV, p. 173.

8   *Ibid.*, vol. XX, p. 460.

9   *Ibid.*, vol. XXVIII, p. 70.

10   *Ibid.*, vol. XXV p. 260

11   M. Vickers, *Reunion Revisited* (Leominster, 2017), pp. 22ff.

12   Michael Rear, *One Step More* (London, 1987), pp. 20ff.

13   *The Memoirs of Gregorio Panzani: Giving an Account of his Agency in England in the Years 1634, 1635, 1636* (London, 2018).

14   G. L. Slosser, *Christian Unity* (London, 1929), p. 109. See also Leopold von Ranke, *A History of England* (London, 1875), vol III, pp. 339–40.

15   J. H. Newman, *A Letter Addressed to the Rev. E. B. Pusey on Occasion of his Eirenicon* (London, 1866), p. 17.

16   *Letters and Diaries*, vol. XXVIII, p. 33.

17   *Ibid.*, p. 18.

18   *Ibid.*, p. 66.

19 *Difficulties*, vol. I, Lecture 3, pp. 81–2.

20 *Documents on Anglican–Roman Catholic Relations*, publ. for the Lambeth Conference (1968), III, 17.

21 Vatican II, *Decree on Ecumenism (Unitatis Redintegratio)*, para. 3, p. 455.

22 Vatican II, *Dogmatic Constitution on the Church (Lumen Gentium)* para. 14, p. 367.

23 Congregation of the Doctrine of the Faith, *Declaration: Dominus Jesus on the Unicity and Salvific Universality of Jesus Christ and the Church* (16 June 2000), n. 56.

24 Vatican II, *Decree on Ecumenism*, para 13, p. 463.

25 Pope St Paul VI, *Allocution on the Beatification of Dominic Barberi* (27 October 1963).

26 *The Guardian*, 13 August 1890.

27 The Preface of this book and *L'Osservatore Romano* (12 October 2019).

Chapter 5

1 See C. Michael Shea, 'Father Giovanni Perrone and Doctrinal Development: An Overlooked Legacy of Newman's Essay on Development', *Journal for the History of Modern Theology* (4 October 2013), pp. 85–116.

2 *Development of Christian Doctrine*, p. 5.

3 Cited in John R. Connolly and Brian W. Hughes, eds., *Newman and Life in the Spirit* (Minneapolis, 2014), p. 51.

4 *Father Giovanni Perrone*, pp. 112–13.

5 Pope Pius IX, *Singulari Quidem* (1856), para. 8.

6 Vatican II, *Dogmatic Constitution on Divine Revelation*, para. 8, p. 754.

7 Joseph Ratzinger, 'The Ecclesiology of the Second Vatican Council', *Communio* 13 (1986), 241–2.

8 Benedict XVI, *Address of His Holiness Benedict XVI to the Roman Curia* (22 December 2005).

9 St Augustine, *On the Literal Meaning of Genesis*, bk. I, ch. 19, para. 39.

10 J. H. Newman, *The Idea of a University* (London, 1947), Discourse 9, 'Duties of the Church towards Knowledge', p. 194.

11 *Letters and Diaries*, vol. XXIV, p. 77.

12 *John Henry Newman, Doctor of the Church*, ed. P. Lefebre and C. Mason (Oxford, 2007), 'The Biglietto Speech', p. 313.

13 J. H. Newman, *The Via Media of the Anglican Church* (Oxford, 1990), pp. 25–6.

14 Avery Dulles, *John Henry Newman* (London, 2002), p. 112.

Chapter 6

1 *Letters and Diaries*, vol. XXV p. 160.

2 Cited in Placid Murray, OSB, *Newman, the Oratorian* (Dublin, 1969), p. 191.

3 Anthony Symondson, SJ, *A Tribute to Fr Frederick William Faber*, New Liturgical Movement (26 September 2013).

4 Jaroslav Pelikan, *The Idea of the University: A Re-examination* (New Haven, 1992), p. 190.

5   *The Idea of a University*, Discourse 5, 'Knowledge its Own End', p. 91.

6   *Ibid.*, Discourse 6, 'Knowledge Viewed in Relation to Learning', pp. 119–20.

7   *Ibid.*, pp. 118–19

8   J. H. Newman, *My Campaign in Ireland, Part I* (Aberdeen, 1896), pp. 119–20.

9   *The Idea of a University*, Discourse 5, 'Knowledge its Own End', pp. 89–90.

10   *Ibid..*, Discourse 7, 'Knowledge Viewed in Relation to Professional Skill', pp. 148–9.

11   *Ibid.*, Discourse 9, 'Duties of the Church towards Knowledge', pp. 205–6.

12   *Ibid.*, Discourse 5, 'Knowledge its Own End', pp. 106–7.

13   J. H. Newman, *The Tamworth Reading Room*, Section 3, 'Discussions and Arguments on Various Subjects' (London, 1891), pp. 272–4.

14   *The Idea of a University*, Discourse 8, 'Knowledge and Religious Duty', p. 170

15   *Ibid.*, Discourse 5, 'Knowledge its own End', p. 88.

16   *Ibid.*, Discourse 2, 'Theology a Branch of Knowledge', p. 24.

17   O. Chadwick, *Newman* (Oxford, 1983), p. 56.

18   A. MacIntyre, 'The Very Idea of a University: Aristotle, Newman, and Us', *British Journal of Educational Studies*, 57/4 (December 2009), pp. 347–62.

19   Breda O'Brien, in *The Irish Times* (6 May 2020).

20   Sophia Deboick, 'Can a University have a Soul?' *The Guardian* (20 October 2019).

21   Cited by Catherine Lough, *Daily Telegraph* (19 November 2022).

22   J. H. Newman, *On Consulting the Faithful in Matters of Doctrine*, ed. J. Coulson (London, 1986), p. 63.

23   *Letters and Diaries*, vol. XIX, p. 545.

24   *On Consulting the Faithful*, p. 114.

25   David Newsome, *The Convert Cardinals* (London, 1993), p. 331.

26   Cited in *On Consulting the Faithful*, pp. 41–2.

27   J. H. Newman, *The Present Position of Catholics in England* (Leominster, 2000), p. 390.

28   *Autobiographical Writings*, pp. 251–6.

29   *Letters and Diaries*, vol. XIX, 179–80.

30   Vatican Council II, *Constitution on the Church*, para. 37, p. 395.

31   The International Theological Commission of the Catholic Church, *Sensus Fidei in the Life of the Church* (2014), para. 3.

32   *Ibid.*, para. 127.

33   Bishop Philip Egan, *Communications from the Catholic Bishops Conference* (27 January 2024).

34   Cited in Newsome, *The Convert Cardinals*, p. 364.

35   Dulles, *John Henry Newman*, p. 163.

36   Ian Ker, *Newman and the Fullness of Christianity* (Edinburgh, 1993), p. 127.

37   B. C. Butler, 'Newman at the Second Vatican Council', in *Rediscovery of Newman*, An Oxford Symposium (London, 1967).

38 Pope Paul VI, *Address to the Participantsin the Cardinal Newman Academic Symposium* (Rome, 7 April 1975).

39 Cardinal Basil Hume, OSB, *Cardinal John Henry Newman, A Saint for our Time?* (London, 1980), p. 3.

40 *Parochial and Plain Sermons*, vol. V, Sermon 15, p. 1084.

41 *Mr. Kingsley and Dr. Newman: A Correspondence on the Question whether Dr. Newman teaches that Truth is no virtue?* (Whitefish, 2008).

42 *Letters and Diaries*, vol. XXI, p. xiii.

43 Cited in I. Ker, *John Henry Newman, a Biography* (Oxford, 1988), p. 692.

44 Henry Edward Manning, *The Present Crisis of the Holy See* (London, 1861), pp.82–3.

45 Henry Edward Manning, *The Temporal Power of the Vicar of Jesus Christ* (London, 1862), p. 74.

46 *Letters and Diaries*, vol. XVIII, p. 300.

47 Henry Edward Manning, *The True Story of the Vatican Council* (London, 1877), p. 4.

48 Cited in Edward Sheridan Purcell, *Life of Cardinal Manning* (London, 1899), p. 323.

49 *Letters and Diaries*, vol. XV, p. 19

50 *The Christian Faith in the Doctrinal Documents of the Catholic Church*, ed. N. Neuner and J. Dupuis (London, 1983), p. 234.

51 Manning, *The Pastoral Office* (1883), p. 218, cited in *Two Cardinals*, p. 364.

52 *Letters and Diaries*, vol. XXV, p. 330.

53 Vatican Council II, *Constitution on the Church*, para. 12, p. 363.

54 J. H. Newman, *Letter to the Duke of Norfolk* (London, 2015), p. 88.

55 *Ibid.*, p. 47.

56 *Ibid.*, p. 50.

57 *Ibid.*, p. 43.

58 *Letter of his Holiness John Paul II to the Archbishop of Birmingham on the First Centenary of the Death of John Henry Newman* (Vatican, 18 June 1990).

59 *Letter to the Duke of Norfolk*, pp. 47–8.

60 *Letters and Diaries*, vol. XXX, p. 207.

61 *Apologia*, p. 25.

62 C. Zaleski, *Newman for a New Generation*, pp. 262ff, cited in F. A. Murphy, ed., *The Beauty of God's House* (Eugene, Oregon, 2014).

63 J. H. Newman, *Fifteen Sermons Preached before the University of Oxford* (Oxford, 2006), Sermon X, pp. 140–1.

64 *Letters and Diaries*, vol. XXV, p. 97.

65 J. H. Newman, *An Essay in Aid of A Grammar of Assent*, ed. I. T. Ker (Oxford, 1985), pp. 273–4.

66 See Logan Paul Gage, 'Newman's Argument from Conscience: Why he needs Paley and natural theology after all', *American Catholic Philosophical Quarterly* 94/1 (2020). Also, Richard Swinburne, *The Existence of God* (London, 2004).

67   *Apologia*, p. 216.

68   Cited in Charlotte Hansen, 'Newman, Conscience and Authority', *New Blackfriars* 92/1038 (2011), p. 209.

69   J. H. Newman, *Callista* (London, 2017), p. 143.

70   *Grammar of Assent*, p. 75–6.

71   *Apologia*, p. 188.

72   *Parochial and Plain Sermons*, vol. I, Sermon 15, p.127.

73   *Grammar of Assent*, p. 73.

74   Paul Shrimpton, *Conscience before Conformity* (Leominster, 2018).

75   Presentation by his Eminence Cardinal Joseph Ratzinger on the occasion of the first centenary of the death of Cardinal John Henry Newman (Rome, 28 April 1990).

76   *Apologia*, p. 218.

77   *Sermons Preached on Various Occasions*, Sermon V, pp. 65–6.

78   *Grammar of Assent*, p. 155.

79   *Ibid.*, p. 300.

80   *Ibid.*, p. 243.

81   *Letters and Diaries*, vol. XXI, p. 146.

82   *Grammar of Assent*, p. 275.

83   Cited in Brian Martin, *John Henry Newman* (London, 1990), p. 152.

84   Aidan Nichols, OP, *A Grammar of Consent* (London, 1991), part 2, ch. 1, 'John Henry Newman and the Illative Sense'.

85   *Development of Christian Doctrine*, p. 27.

86   *Catechism of the Catholic Church*, para. 15.

87   *Grammar of Assent*, pp. 65–6.

88   *Parochial and Plain Sermons*, vol. VII, Sermon 10, p. 1484.

89   *Grammar of Assent*, p. 321.

90   *Ibid.*, p. 270.

91   *Discourses Addressed to Mixed Congregations*, p. 49.

92   *Grammar of Assent*, p. 316.

93   https://youtu.be/cP_eL7FiIXk?t=12

94   *Parochial and Plain Sermons*, vol. III, Sermon 6, p. 531.

95   *Ibid.*, vol. VI, Sermon 18, p. 1337.

96   *Apologia*, p. 214–5.

97   *Fifteen Sermons*, Sermon 13, p. 251.

98   *Ibid.*, Sermon 15, pp. 312–13.

99   J. H. Newman, *Lectures on the Doctrine of Justification*, 3rd edn (Eugene, Oregon, 2001), p. 175.

100   *Ibid.*, p. 172.

101   *Ibid.*, p. 120.

102   *Parochial and Plain Sermons*, vol. I, Sermon 13, pp. 109–10.

103   *Ibid.*, vol. IV, Sermon 22, p. 935.

104 *Ibid.,* vol. VI, Sermon 15, p. 1313.

105 *Ibid.,* vol. VI, Sermon 11, p. 1271.

106 *Ibid.,* vol. IV, Sermon 14, p. 866.

Chapter 7

1 *Letters and Diaries,* vol. XIX, p. xv.

2 *The Convert Cardinals,* p. 346.

3 *Letters and Diaries,* vol. XXIX, p. 419.

4 *John Henry Newman, Doctor of the Church,* p. 313.

5 J. H. Newman, *The Church of the Fathers* (Leominster, 2002), p. 1.

Chapter 8

1 *Letters and Diaries,* vol. XIII, p. 419.

2 Cited in Dessain, *John Henry Newman,* pp. 166–7.

3 Cited in Martin, *John Henry Newman,* p. 138.

4 *Parochial and Plain Sermons,* vol. III, Sermon 24, p. 706.

5 Cited in Murray, *Newman, the Oratorian,* p. 59–62.

6 Cited in F. Horner, *Time Remembered* (London, 1933), p. 120.

7 *Discourses Addressed to Mixed Congregations,* p. 31.

8 *Parochial and Plain Sermons,* vol. VIII, Sermon 2, p. 1574.

9 Cited in Joyce Sugg, *Ever Yours Affly: John Henry Newman and his Female Circle* (Leominster, 1996) p. 298.

Chapter 9

1 Cited in Peter Jennings, ed., *Benedict XVI and Cardinal Newman* (Oxford, 2005), p. 35.

INDEX OF THEMES AND TOPICS

www.ingramcontent.com/pod-product-compliance
Lightning Source LLC
Chambersburg PA
CBHW022026090426
42739CB00006BA/308